EASY-TO-MAKE PATCHWORK SKIRTS

Step-by-Step Instructions and Full-Size Templates for 12 Skirts & 2 Aprons

NANCY PFEIFFER

Dover Publications, Inc.
New York

Copyright © 1980 by Nancy Pfeiffer.
All rights reserved under Pan American and International Copyright Conventions.

Published in Canada by General Publishing Company, Ltd., 30 Lesmill Road, Don Mills, Toronto, Ontario.
Published in the United Kingdom by Constable and Company, Ltd., 10 Orange Street, London WC2H 7EG.

Easy-to-Make Patchwork Skirts is a new work, first published by Dover Publications, Inc., in 1980.

International Standard Book Number: 0-486-23888-1
Library of Congress Catalog Card Number: 79-53930

Manufactured in the United States of America
Dover Publications, Inc.
180 Varick Street
New York, N.Y. 10014

Introduction

In our modern machine age when department stores sell inexpensive and beautiful bed coverings, we may no longer need to use patchwork to make quilts. We can, however, still know the joy of creating a beautiful piece of patchwork by using the medium for other crafts. Although patchwork originated as a utilitarian craft, its innate beauty makes it especially applicable to other decorative projects. One of the most delightful of these is the patchwork skirt.

This book contains full-size templates and complete instructions for making twelve patchwork skirts and two patchwork aprons. If you have always wanted to learn how to do patchwork but have not wanted to undertake the making of an entire quilt as a first project, these skirts will serve as a good introduction to the craft. Many of the designs are based upon traditional quilt blocks. Once you have mastered the technique of working with patchwork by making a skirt, you may want to use the templates to make a quilt by making and joining additional quilt blocks.

Before beginning to work on the skirt of your choice, read through the general instructions on skirt making. As you work through your skirt, refer back to these instructions for guidance.

TEMPLATES

All of the pattern pieces used in making these skirts are given in actual-size templates printed on heavyweight paper in the template section of this book. Locate the designated template and carefully cut it out. It is important that all templates be cut out carefully because if they are not accurate, the patchwork pieces will not fit together. Use a pair of good-sized sharp scissors, a single-edged razor blade or an X-Acto knife. Be careful not to blunt the fine corners of the triangles.

CHOICE OF MATERIALS

The skirts illustrated were all made of cotton blends to make them lightweight and washable. Other fabrics such as satins and velvets can be used to give an elegant effect that is especially appropriate for evening wear. Because skirts are not likely to get the hard wear quilts do, thin fabrics such as batiste and dotted swiss can also be employed.

If the skirt is to be washable, check all fabrics to make certain that they are both colorfast and preshrunk. You *can* rely on the manufacturers' labels, but the safest method is to wash all fabrics in very hot water before using them. Be especially wary of reds and dark blues which tend to bleed if the original dyeing was not done with care. All new materials should be washed to remove any sizing.

The color schemes specified are only meant as guidelines. Feel free to use your own color choices. When choosing fabrics, it is probably easiest to first choose a dominant print or striped fabric. The other fabrics can then be plain, checked or other prints that pick up the colors of the dominant fabric.

At the beginning of each skirt I have indicated the amount of 40" material you will need to complete a skirt. More fabric will be needed for material which is less than 40" wide. Yardage is also calculated for skirts not longer than 40". If your skirt is to be longer than 40", some additional fabric will be required. Generally, the amount of fabric for strips or bands is given without piecing. Less material will be needed if you prefer to piece the strips.

DESIGNS

Authorities have differing opinions as to how wide a skirt should be. Some say 1 1/2 times your waist and some say 1 1/2 times your hip measurement. The skirts in this book are generally 54" to 64" wide and should fit most people who wear sizes 12-16. All of the skirts can be made longer or shorter—and in most cases narrower or wider—by altering the designs slightly. On an all-over design, the rows of blocks can be increased or decreased to give the needed length or width. Blocks can be added to make a skirt wider or subtracted to make it narrower. The width of strips at the top or bottom can also be adjusted to shorten or lengthen the skirt. When figuring the width of a bottom strip, be sure to add 3 1/4" to allow for a 2 1/2" hem, 3/8" seam allowance when attaching the band to the rest of the skirt and 3/8" to turn under when finishing the hem.

CUTTING THE FABRIC

Cutting is one of the most important steps in making any kind of patchwork. You must be accurate in order to have the pattern fit perfectly.

Press all fabric to remove wrinkles and crease marks. Check the grain line of the fabric carefully. Lengthwise threads should be parallel to the selvage and crosswise threads exactly perpendicular to the selvage to insure that the pieces will be correctly cut. (See figure 1.) If the fabric seems off-grain, pull it gently to straighten it. Do this on the true bias in the opposite direction to the off-grain edge. Continue this stretching until the crosswise threads are at right angles to the lengthwise threads. (See figure 2.)

Lay the fabric on a large, smooth surface with the wrong side up. Have all of your supplies ready: scissors, ruler, sharp pencils and the appropriate templates.

You will notice that the templates include a 3/8'' seam allowance. Traditionally quilts are made with a 1/4'' seam allowance, but I have found the 3/8'' seam allowance to be more practical, especially if you are using the sewing machine. Sewing plates on most machines are marked off for seam allowances, and the smallest measurement is 3/8''. You can cut your pieces with this seam allowance and, by using that measurement on your plate, sew with a perfect sewing line. Place the template on the fabric and then trace around the template with a well-sharpened, hard lead pencil; use a light-colored pencil or tailor's chalk for dark fabrics and a regular lead pencil for light fabrics. Hold the pencil at an angle so that the point of the pencil is against the edge of the template.

If you are planning to sew your pieces by hand, you may prefer cutting off the seam allowance on the template. Then trace around the template with the pencil. Now measure 3/8'' around this shape. Using a ruler, draw this second line. This is the line that you will cut on. Now you will see that the first line (where you traced the template) is there to use as a guide for the stitching. The seam allowance does not have to be perfect, but the sewing line must be perfectly straight and true, or the pieces will not fit together into a perfectly shaped design.

I often combine the two techniques when cutting for hand sewing. First I trace around the template with the seam allowance to give me the cutting line. Then I cut the seam allowance off the template and lay this smaller template in the center of the cut fabric piece and trace around it to get the sewing line.

Continue moving the template and tracing it on the fabric the required number of times, moving from left to right and always keeping the straight sides parallel with the grain. Try to keep the triangles on the true bias of the fabric by placing the short sides of the triangles on the straight of the fabric. (See figure 3.) You will conserve fabric by letting pieces share a common cutting line, but if this is confusing leave a narrow border or margin around each piece. A piece of felt placed under the fabric will help to keep it from slipping as you are marking the pieces.

When cutting fabric that is to be used for both strips and blocks, cut the strips first; then cut the patches from the remaining material. Whenever possible strips should be cut lengthwise along the selvage edge. When necessary strips may be pieced to get the desired length.

ASSEMBLING THE BLOCK

It is best to begin by first sewing the pieces into blocks wherever this is indicated in the instructions. Place two pieces together with the right sides facing. Pieces which

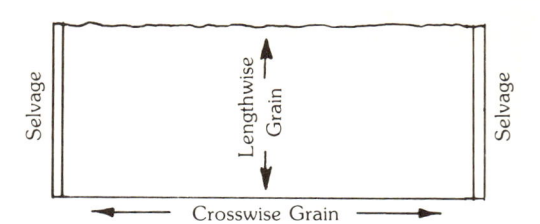

Figure 1. Lengthwise threads should be parallel to the selvage and crosswise threads perpendicular to the selvage.

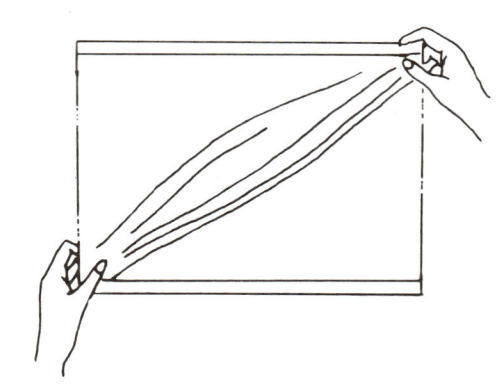

Figure 2. Pull fabric on the true bias in the opposite direction to the off-grain edge to straigthen the fabric.

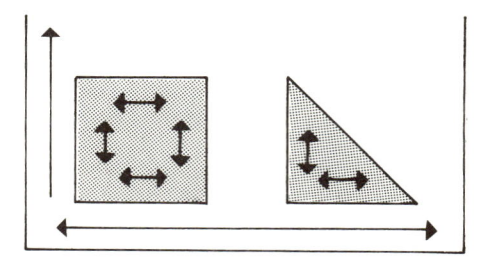

Figure 3. Place templates on the fabric so that as many straight sides of the pattern as possible are parallel to the crosswise and lengthwise grain of the fabric.

are to be machine sewn should be carefully placed so that the top edges of both pieces are even. If you are planning to sew by hand, place a pin through both pieces at each end of the sewing line. Check on the back to make sure that the pins are exactly on the pencil line. When sewing larger seams, place pins every 1 1/2'', and remove them as you sew past them. Always stitch on the sewing line, being very careful not to stitch into the seam allowance at the corners.

After you join two pieces together, press the seams flat to one side—not open. As a rule, seams should all be pressed in the same direction, but darker pieces should not be pressed so that they will fall under the lighter pieces since they may show through when the skirt is completed. All seams should be pressed before they are crossed with another seam. To keep seams from bunching, clip away excess fabric, if necessary, at these crossing points. It is best to finish the seam edges of any fabric—such as dotted swiss—that may tend to fray easily.

Place the completed block on the ironing board and pull the edges of the block straight with your fingers. After making sure that the block is perfectly square, place pins in the corners and at several places along the edges to hold it rigidly in place. Cover the block with a damp cloth and steam with a warm iron (or use a steam iron). Do not let the pressing cloth get dry. Iron the edges until they are perfectly square and of equal measurements. The center is ironed last. The block should be ironed perfectly flat with no pucker.

ASSEMBLING THE SKIRT

After you have assembled the required number of blocks, refer to the skirt diagram and assemble the skirt. Beginning at either the top or bottom, sew the strips to each other and/or to the blocks, being careful to match patterns where necessary. Continue pressing all seams closed in one direction. Finish any seams which may have a tendency to fray.

When the skirt has been assembled, iron it in the same manner as you ironed the individual blocks.

LINING

Measure the completed skirt to check your measurements before you cut your lining fabric. The measurements given with the instructions for each skirt are strictly mathematical. They do not allow for variations that can occur as you work with fabric which can shrink or stretch. Do not be concerned with any slight variations in size; just prepare your lining according to the new measurements.

After carefully ironing the pieced skirt, sew the ends of the skirt together. Sew the ends of the lining together. Lay the wrong side of the lining on the wrong side of the skirt with the top edges of the skirt and lining even. Sew the skirt and the lining together 1/4" from this top edge. If you plan to use a zipper in your skirt, be sure to leave the appropriate opening in both the skirt and the lining. After the skirt is completed, hem it and the lining separately. The lining should be slightly shorter than the skirt.

FINISHING THE SKIRT

Skirts wider than 56" look better finished with a waistband, as elastic casing makes for a rather fully gathered skirt. Skirts under 56" can be finished with either a waistband or elastic casing.

Elastic Casing

Sew the ends of the casing strip together. Fold the casing strip in half lengthwise, wrong sides together, and iron along the fold line. Right sides together, pin one edge of the casing strip to the top edge of the skirt. Sew along the 3/8" seam allowance. Fold under the unsewn edge of the casing strip 3/8" and slip stitch this folded edge to the wrong side of the skirt to make a tunnel or casing for the elastic. Leave an opening through which to work the elastic. Cut a piece of 3/4" or 1" elastic to the person's waist measurement plus 1". Insert the elastic through the casing and adjust to fit. Sew the ends of the elastic together and sew the opening closed.

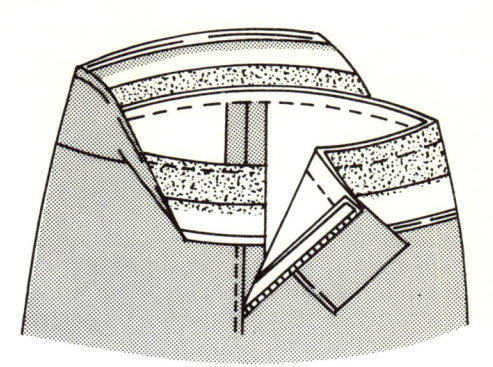

Figure 4. Sew the skirt to the waistband. Trim the seam and press toward the waistband.

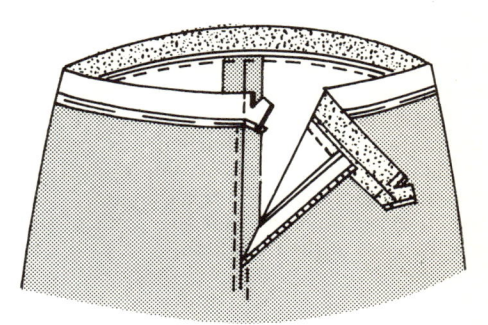

Figure 5. Fold the waistband, stitch the ends and trim.

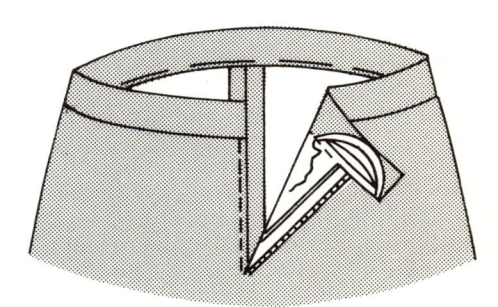

Figure 6. Turn the waistband and slipstitch the unfinished edge over the seam and the extension edges.

Waistband

Cut the waistband 3 3/4" wide by the person's waist measurement plus 3". Insert the zipper in the back opening, following the directions on the zipper package. Gather the skirt to fit the waist. Right sides facing, sew the waistband to the skirt. Trim the seam and press toward the waistband. (See figure 4.) Fold the waistband, stitch the ends and trim. (See figure 5.) Turn the waistband and slipstitch the unfinished edge over the seam and the extension edges together. (See figure 6.) Fasten the waistband with hooks and eyes, if desired.

FINISHING THE APRON

Fold the waistband and ties in half lengthwise, and turn under 3/8" along both long raw edges. Fold the waistband in half crosswise to find the center. Pin the center of the waistband to the center of the apron. Sew the waistband to the apron and finish the ties.

v

EASY-TO-MAKE PATCHWORK SKIRTS

Hope of Hartford Skirt

MATERIALS AND EQUIPMENT

Skirt fabric: 2 yards light blue; 1 1/2 yards white print; 1/2 yard brown print.
Lining fabric: 1 3/4 yards.
Sharp scissors, pencils, straight pins, needles, zipper or elastic, sewing thread.

DIRECTIONS

Before beginning the skirt, read the general directions on pages iii to v.
1. Cut out the appropriate templates on plates 1 and 2.
2. Cut out the required pieces listed below.
3. Following the block diagram, sew the pieces into eight blocks.
4. Following the skirt diagram, assemble the blocks and strips.
5. Measure the completed skirt and cut the lining material to match.
6. Sew the sides of the skirt together, and sew the sides of the lining together. If you are planning to use a zipper in the skirt, be sure to leave the appropriate opening at the top.
7. Lay the wrong side of the lining on the wrong side of the skirt with the top edges of the skirt and lining even. Sew the skirt and lining together 1/4" from this top edge.
8. Following the directions in the introduction, apply either the elastic casing or the waistband to the skirt.
9. Hem skirt and lining separately.

NUMBER OF PIECES TO BE CUT

Piece No. 1 .... 32 White Print
Piece No. 2 .... 32 Brown Print
Piece No. 2 .... 32 Light Blue
Piece No. 3 .... 8 Brown Print
Piece No. 4 .... 32 Light Blue
Strip A (2 1/4" × 12 1/2") .... 8 Light Blue
Strip B (3 3/4" × 54 3/4") .... 2 Light Blue
Strip B (3 3/4" × 54 3/4") .... 2 White Print
Strip C (54 3/4" × sufficient width to give desired length plus 3 1/4" for hem) .... 1 Light Blue
Waistband (3 3/4" × the desired length) ..... 1 Light Blue
or
Elastic Casing (3 1/4" × 54 3/4") .... 1 Light Blue

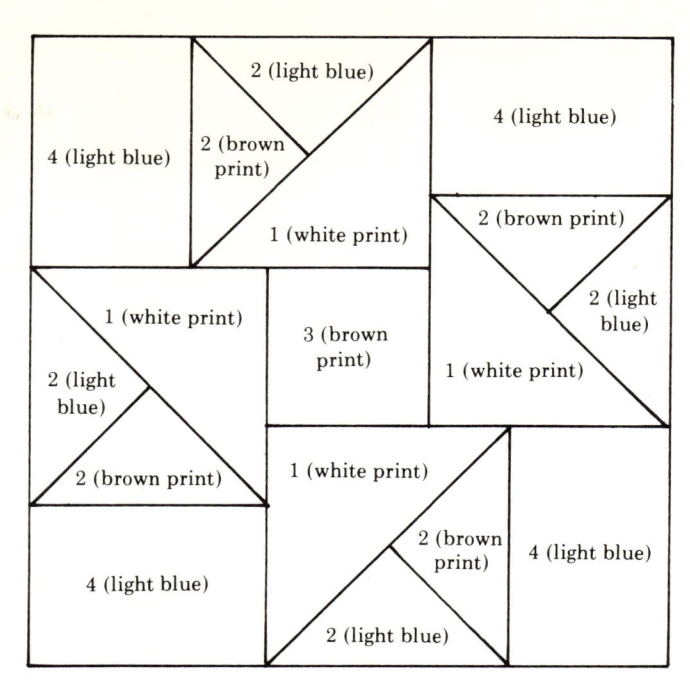

BLOCK DIAGRAM

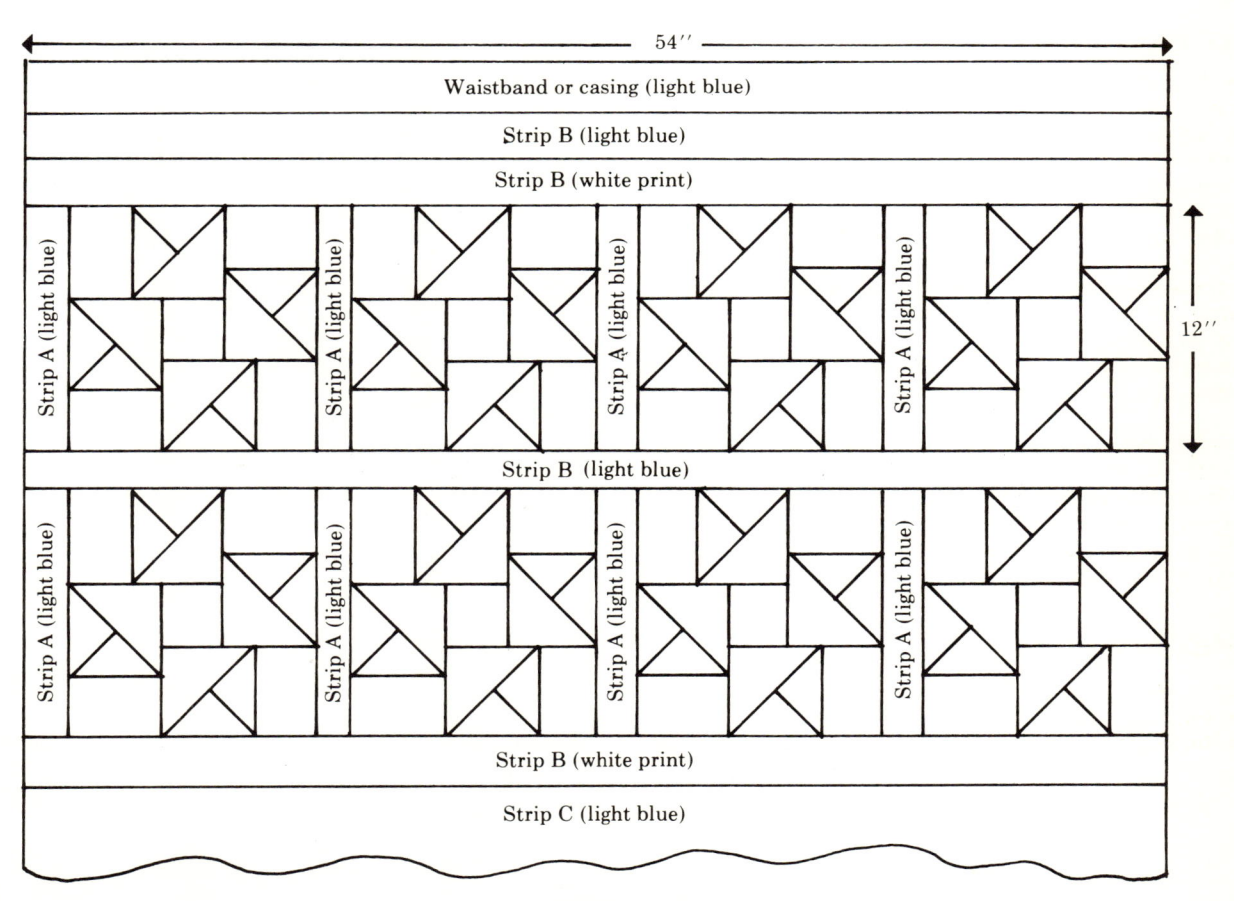

- 4 (light blue)
- 2 (light blue)
- 2 (brown print)
- 1 (white print)
- 4 (light blue)
- 2 (brown print)
- 2 (light blue)
- 1 (white print)
- 2 (light blue)
- 3 (brown print)
- 1 (white print)
- 2 (brown print)
- 1 (white print)
- 4 (light blue)
- 2 (brown print)
- 4 (light blue)
- 2 (light blue)

SKIRT DIAGRAM

54″

- Waistband or casing (light blue)
- Strip B (light blue)
- Strip B (white print)
- Strip A (light blue) [repeated]
- Strip B (light blue)
- Strip A (light blue) [repeated]
- Strip B (white print)
- Strip C (light blue)

12″

Spider Web Skirt

MATERIALS AND EQUIPMENT

Skirt fabric: 3 yards dark brown; 3/4 yard orange print; 1/3 yard orange; 1/3 yard orange dotted swiss.
Lining fabric: 1 3/4 yards.
Sharp scissors, pencils, straight pins, needles, zipper or elastic, sewing thread.

DIRECTIONS

Before beginning the skirt, read the general directions on pages iii to v.
1. Cut out the appropriate templates on plates 2 and 3.
2. Cut out the required pieces listed below.
3. Following the diagram for Block I, sew the pieces into eight blocks.
4. Following the diagram for Block II, sew the pieces into seven blocks.
5. Following the skirt diagram, assemble the blocks and strips. Notice that Strip A is the center front of the skirt.
6. Measure the completed skirt and cut the lining material to match.
7. Sew the sides of the skirt together, and sew the sides of the lining together. If you are planning to use a zipper in the skirt, be sure to leave the appropriate opening at the top.
8. Lay the wrong side of the lining on the wrong side of the skirt with the top edges of the skirt and lining even. Sew the skirt and lining together 1/4″ from this top edge.
9. Following the directions in the introduction, apply either the elastic casing or the waistband to the skirt.
10. Hem skirt and lining separately.

NUMBER OF PIECES TO BE CUT

Piece No. 1 ....60 Dark Brown
Piece No. 2 ....60 Orange Print
Piece No. 3 ....30 Orange
Piece No. 3 ....30 Orange Dotted Swiss
Strip A (5 3/4″ × the desired length plus
　3 3/4″ for hem) ....1 Dark Brown
Strip B (55 3/4″ × sufficient width to give
　desired length plus 3 1/4″ for hem) ......1 Dark Brown
Waistband (3 3/4″ × the desired length) ...1 Dark Brown
　　　　　　　　　　or
Elastic Casing (3 1/4″ × 55″) ....1 Dark Brown

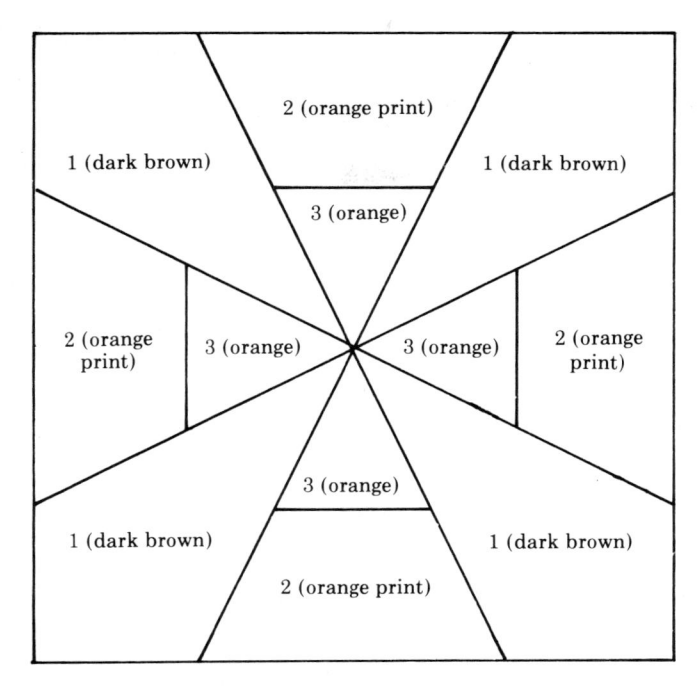

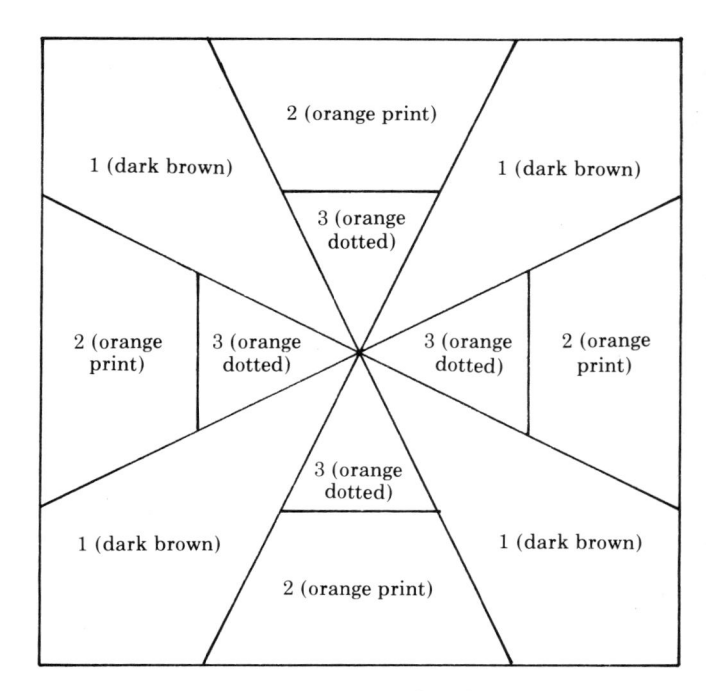

BLOCK I DIAGRAM

- 1 (dark brown)
- 2 (orange print)
- 3 (orange)

BLOCK II DIAGRAM

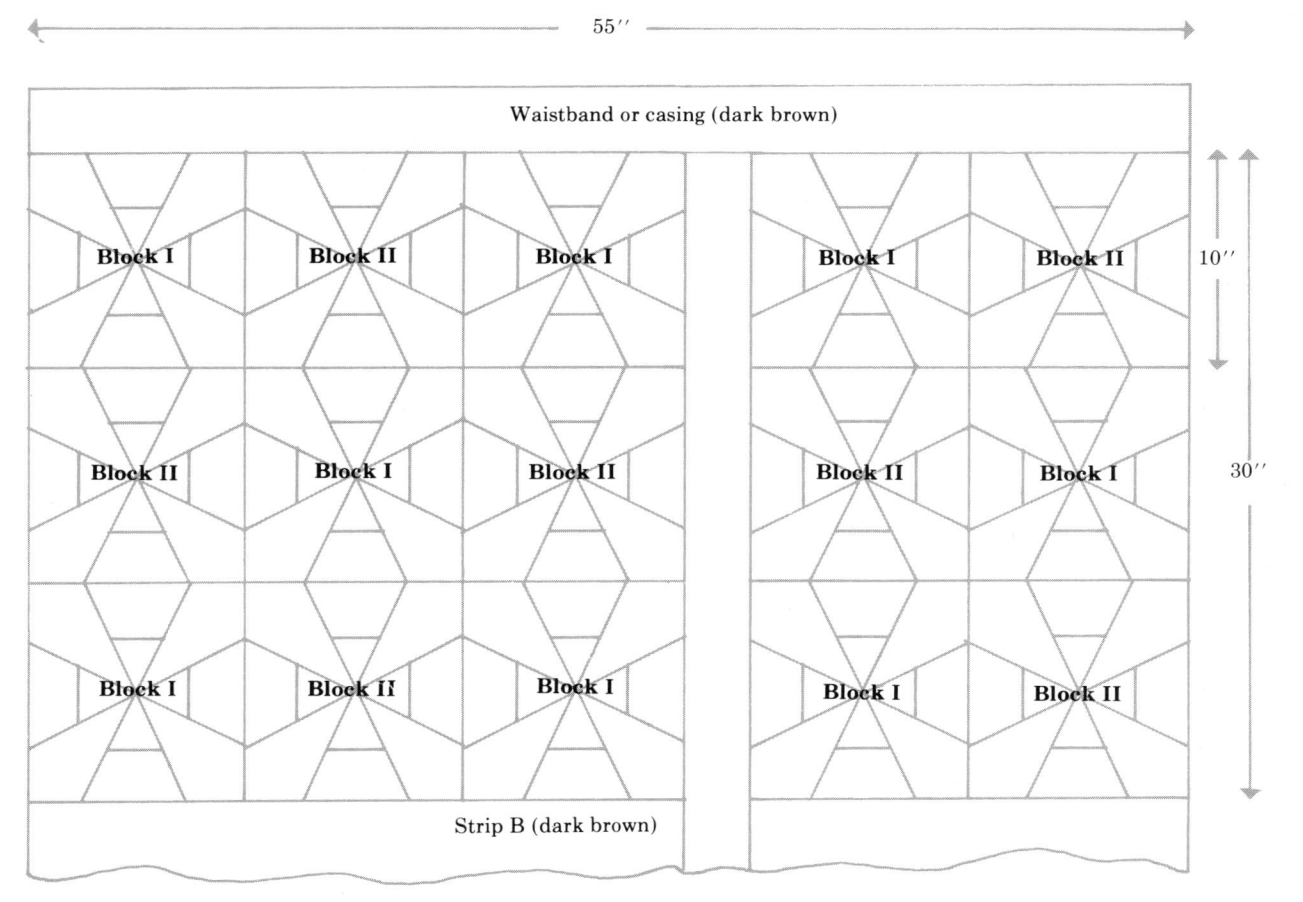

- 1 (dark brown)
- 2 (orange print)
- 3 (orange dotted)

SKIRT DIAGRAM

55″

Waistband or casing (dark brown)

10″

30″

Strip B (dark brown)

Skirt of Many Colors

MATERIALS AND EQUIPMENT

Skirt fabric: 5/8 yard red; 1 yard green; 5/8 yard pink; 5/8 yard orange; 5/8 yard blue; 1/4 yard red print; 1/4 yard green print; 1/4 yard pink print; 1/4 yard orange print; 1/4 yard blue print.
Lining fabric: 1 7/8 yards.
Sharp scissors, pencils, straight pins, needles, zipper, sewing thread.

DIRECTIONS

Before beginning the skirt, read the general directions on pages iii to v.
1. Cut out the appropriate templates on plates 4 and 5.
2. Cut out the required pieces listed below.
3. Following the skirt diagram, assemble the five patchwork strips.
4. Following the skirt diagram, assemble the solid strips and the patchwork strips.
5. Measure the completed skirt and cut the lining material to match.
6. Sew the sides of the skirt together, and sew the sides of the lining together. Be sure to leave the appropriate opening at the top for the zipper.
7. Lay the wrong side of the lining on the wrong side of the skirt with the top edges of the skirt and lining even. Sew the skirt and lining together 1/4″ from this top edge.
8. Following the directions in the introduction, apply the waistband to the skirt.
9. Hem the skirt and the lining separately.

NUMBER OF PIECES TO BE CUT

Piece No. 1 . . . . 7 Red (R)
Piece No. 1 . . . . 7 Green (G)
Piece No. 1 . . . . 7 Pink (P)
Piece No. 1 . . . . 7 Orange (O)
Piece No. 1 . . . . 7 Blue (B)
Piece No. 2 . . . . 12 Red Print (RP)
Piece No. 2 . . . . 12 Green Print (GP)
Piece No. 2 . . . . 12 Pink Print (PP)
Piece No. 2 . . . . 12 Orange Print (OP)
Piece No. 2 . . . . 12 Blue Print (BP)
Piece No. 3 . . . . 4 Red Print (RP)
Piece No. 3 . . . . 4 Green Print (GP)
Piece No. 3 . . . . 4 Pink Print (PP)
Piece No. 3 . . . . 4 Orange Print (OP)
Piece No. 3 . . . . 4 Blue Print (BP)
Solid Strip (6 3/4″ × the desired length plus 3 3/4″ for hem) . . . . 1 Red
Solid Strip . . . . 1 Green
Solid Strip . . . . 1 Pink
Solid Strip . . . . 1 Orange
Solid Strip . . . . 1 Blue
Waistband (3 3/4″ × the desired length) . . . . 1 Green

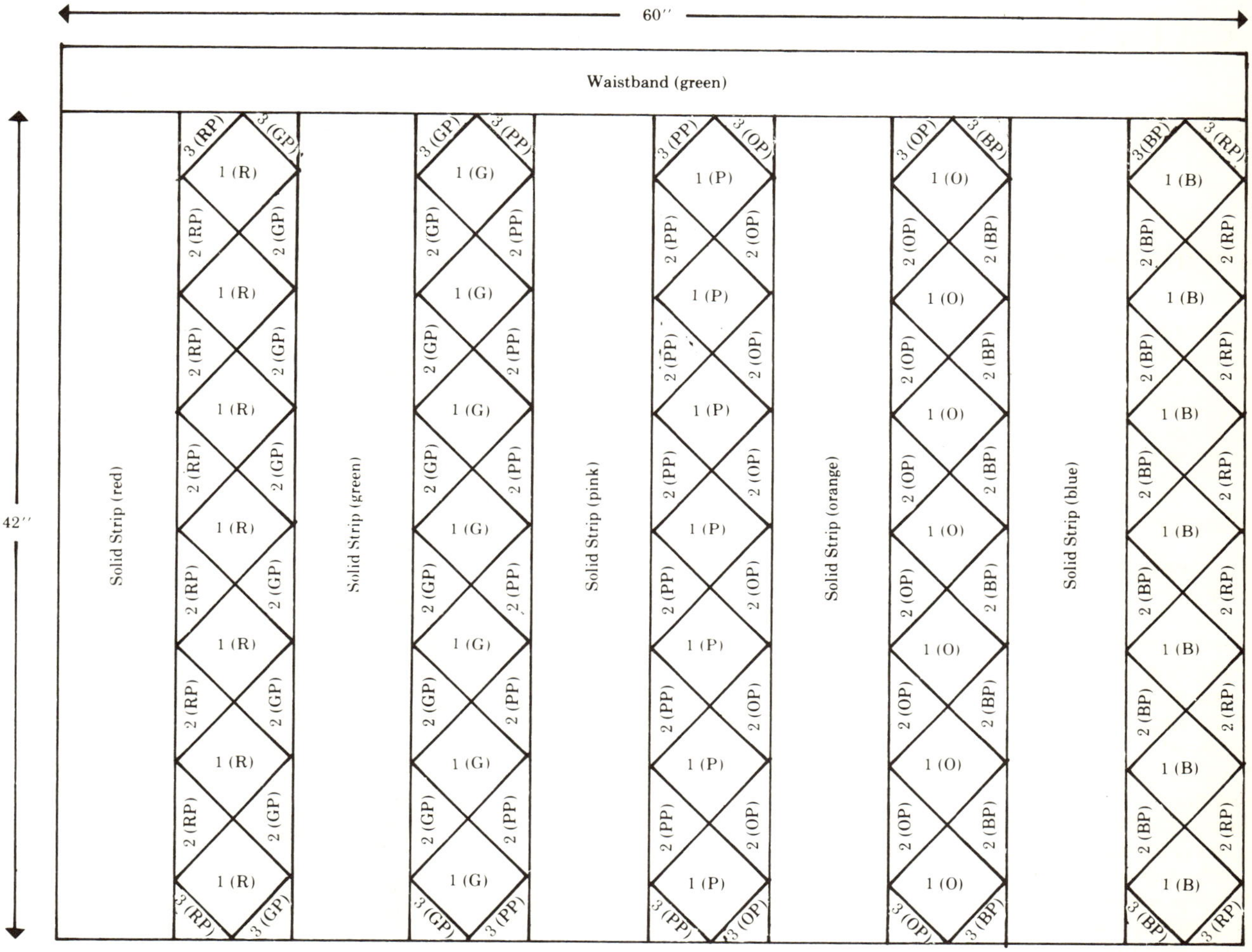
60″
Waistband (green)
42″
Solid Strip (red)
3 (RP)
3 (GP)
1 (R)
2 (RP)
2 (GP)
Solid Strip (green)
3 (GP)
3 (PP)
1 (G)
2 (GP)
2 (PP)
Solid Strip (pink)
3 (PP)
3 (OP)
1 (P)
2 (PP)
2 (OP)
Solid Strip (orange)
3 (OP)
3 (BP)
1 (O)
2 (OP)
2 (BP)
Solid Strip (blue)
3 (BP)
3 (RP)
1 (B)
2 (BP)
2 (RP)

Hexagon Skirt

MATERIALS AND EQUIPMENT

Skirt fabric: 5/8 yard orange print; 1 yard green check; 3/8 yard brown calico; 3/8 yard yellow calico; 3/8 yard green print; 3/8 yard orange check; 1/2 yard yellow print; 1/2 yard brown print.
Lining fabric: 1 3/4 yards.
Sharp scissors, pencils, straight pins, needles, zipper, sewing thread.

DIRECTIONS

Before beginning the skirt, read the general directions on pages iii to v.
1. Cut out the appropriate templates on plates 6 and 7.
2. Cut out the required pieces listed below.
3. Following the skirt diagram, assemble the hexagons.
4. Measure the completed skirt and cut the lining material to match.
5. Sew the sides of the skirt together, and sew the sides of the lining together. Be sure to leave the appropriate opening at the top for the zipper.
6. Lay the wrong side of the lining on the wrong side of the skirt with the top edges of the skirt and lining even. Sew the skirt and lining together 1/4" from this top edge.
7. Following the directions in the introduction, apply the waistband to the skirt.
8. Hem the skirt and the lining separately.

Note: If the desired skirt length is longer than 37", add another row of hexagons to the bottom. Make this row out of the yellow and brown calico. Add an additional 1/4 yard of each fabric to the yardage requirements.

NUMBER OF PIECES TO BE CUT

Piece No. 1 . . . . .6 Yellow Print (YP)
Piece No. 1 . . . . .6 Brown Print (BP)
Piece No. 2 . . . . .12 Orange Print (OP)
Piece No. 2 . . . . .12 Green Check (GC)
Piece No. 2 . . . . .6 Brown Calico (BC)
Piece No. 2 . . . . .6 Yellow Calico (YC)
Piece No. 2 . . . . .6 Green Print (GP)
Piece No. 2 . . . . .6 Orange Check (OC)
Piece No. 2 . . . . .6 Yellow Print (YP)
Piece No. 2 . . . . .6 Brown Print (BP)
Waistband (3 3/4" × the desired length) . . . 1 Green Check

| 60″ wide × 41″ tall layout |

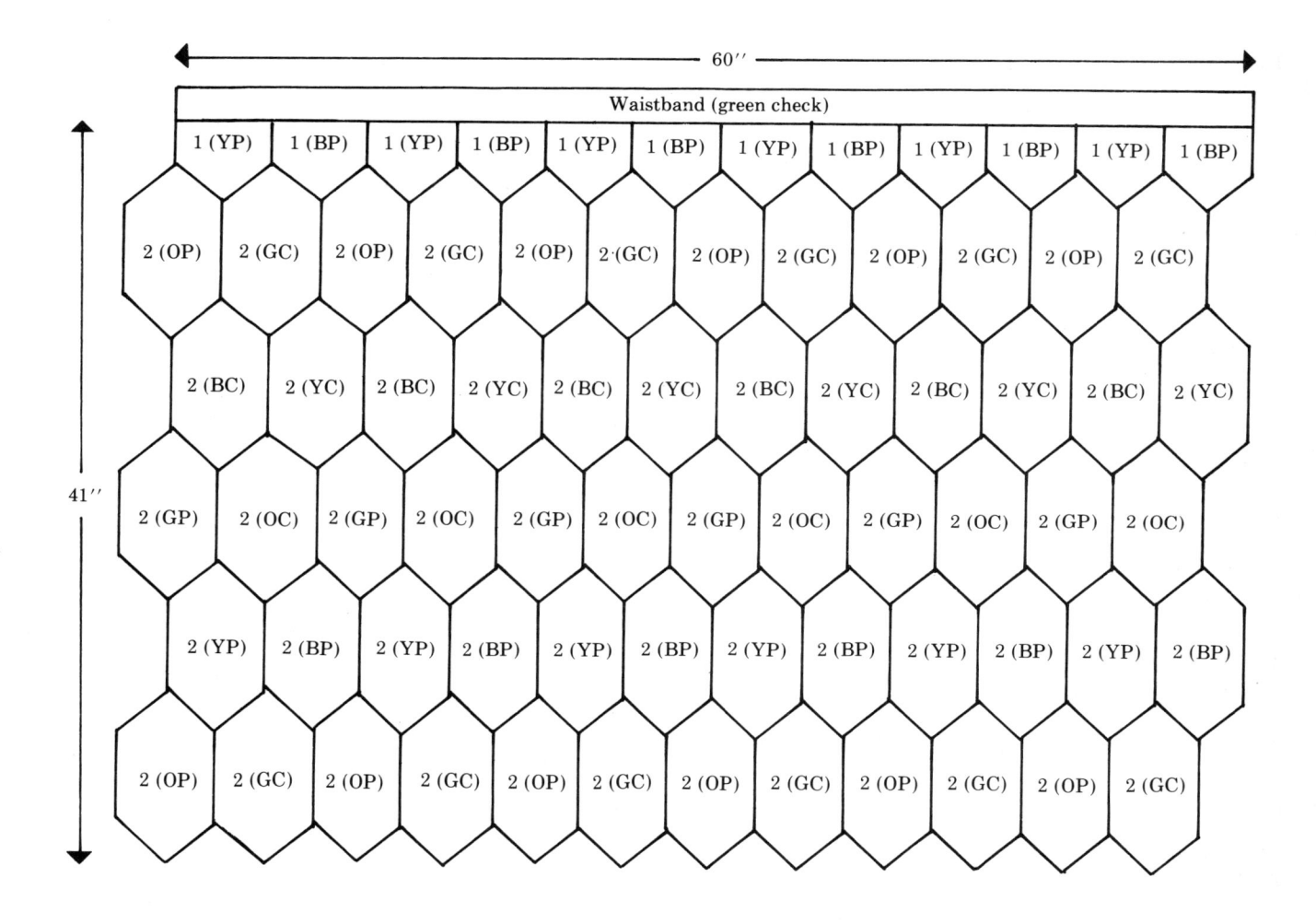

Waistband (green check)

Row 1: 1 (YP) | 1 (BP) | 1 (YP) | 1 (BP) | 1 (YP) | 1 (BP) | 1 (YP) | 1 (BP) | 1 (YP) | 1 (BP) | 1 (YP) | 1 (BP)

Row 2: 2 (OP) | 2 (GC) | 2 (OP) | 2 (GC) | 2 (OP) | 2 (GC) | 2 (OP) | 2 (GC) | 2 (OP) | 2 (GC) | 2 (OP) | 2 (GC)

Row 3: 2 (BC) | 2 (YC) | 2 (BC) | 2 (YC) | 2 (BC) | 2 (YC) | 2 (BC) | 2 (YC) | 2 (BC) | 2 (YC) | 2 (BC) | 2 (YC)

Row 4: 2 (GP) | 2 (OC) | 2 (GP) | 2 (OC) | 2 (GP) | 2 (OC) | 2 (GP) | 2 (OC) | 2 (GP) | 2 (OC) | 2 (GP) | 2 (OC)

Row 5: 2 (YP) | 2 (BP) | 2 (YP) | 2 (BP) | 2 (YP) | 2 (BP) | 2 (YP) | 2 (BP) | 2 (YP) | 2 (BP) | 2 (YP) | 2 (BP)

Row 6: 2 (OP) | 2 (GC) | 2 (OP) | 2 (GC) | 2 (OP) | 2 (GC) | 2 (OP) | 2 (GC) | 2 (OP) | 2 (GC) | 2 (OP) | 2 (GC)

Monkey Wrench Apron

MATERIALS AND EQUIPMENT

Apron fabric: 7/8 yard blue; 3/8 yard red print; 1/4 yard yellow print.
Sharp scissors, pencils, straight pins, needles, sewing thread.

DIRECTIONS

Before beginning the apron, read the general directions on pages iii to v.
1. Cut out the appropriate templates on plate 14.
2. Cut out the required pieces listed below.
3. Following the diagram for Block I, sew the pieces into three blocks.
4. Following the diagram for Block II, sew the pieces into three blocks.
5. Following the apron diagram, assemble the blocks.
6. Sew the hemming strip to the bottom of the apron and turn under for a hem.
7. Make a narrow hem along both sides.
8. Following the directions in the introduction apply the waistband and ties.

NUMBER OF PIECES TO BE CUT

Piece No. 1 .... 24 Blue
Piece No. 1 .... 24 Red Print
Piece No. 2 .... 3 Blue
Piece No. 2 .... 27 Yellow Print
Piece No. 3 .... 24 Blue
Waistband and Ties (3 3/4" × 70 3/4") .... 1 Blue
Hemming Strip (2 1/4" × 30 1/4") .... 1 Blue

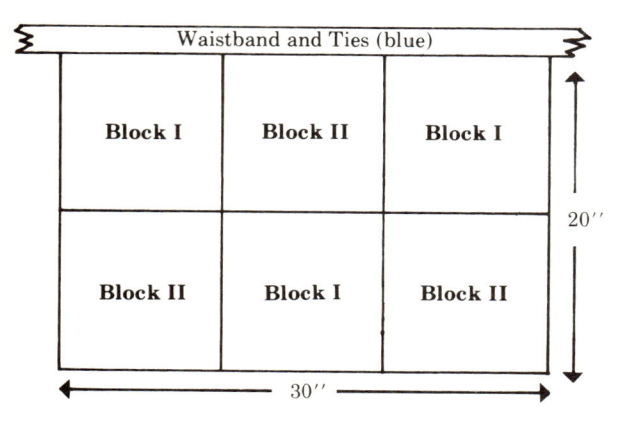

APRON DIAGRAM

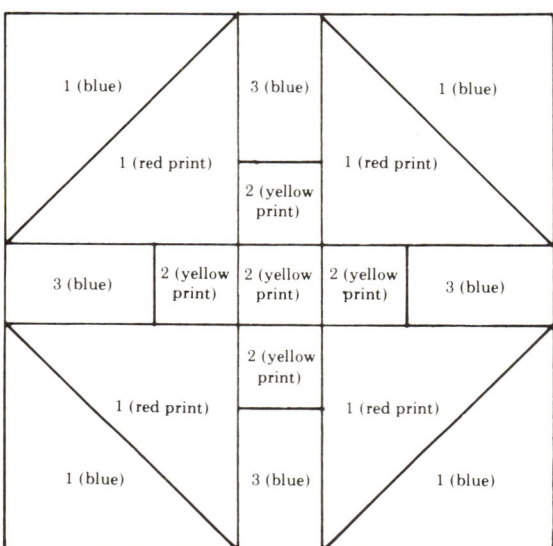

BLOCK I DIAGRAM

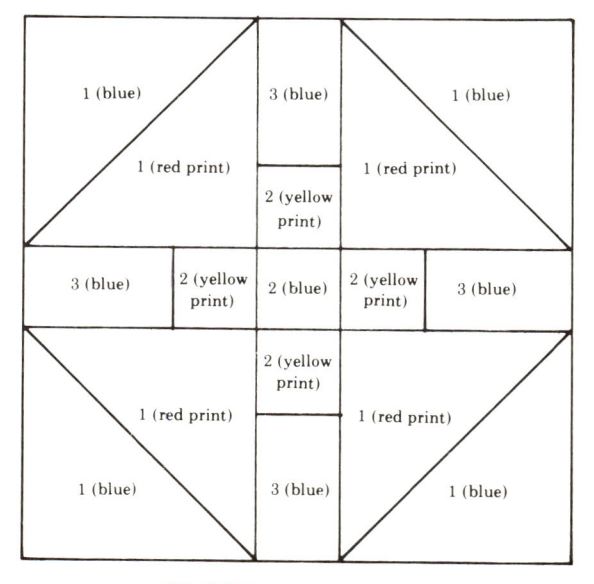

BLOCK II DIAGRAM

Projects continue following templates.

seam allowance

HOPE OF HARTFORD SKIRT
Piece No. 1

HOPE OF HARTFORD SKIRT
Piece No. 2

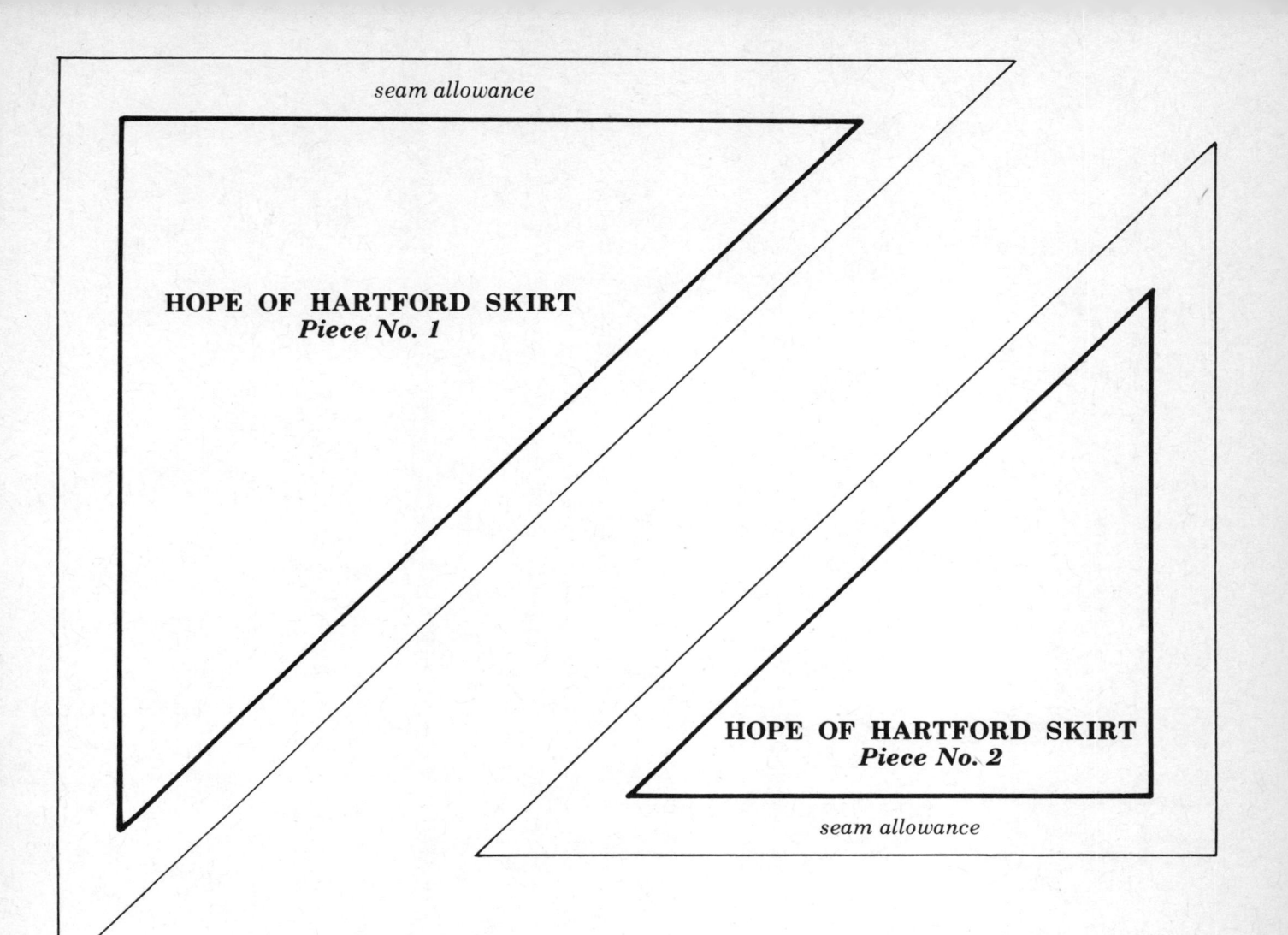

seam allowance

HOPE OF HARTFORD SKIRT
Piece No. 3

seam allowance

PLATE 1

seam allowance

HOPE OF HARTFORD SKIRT
Piece No. 4

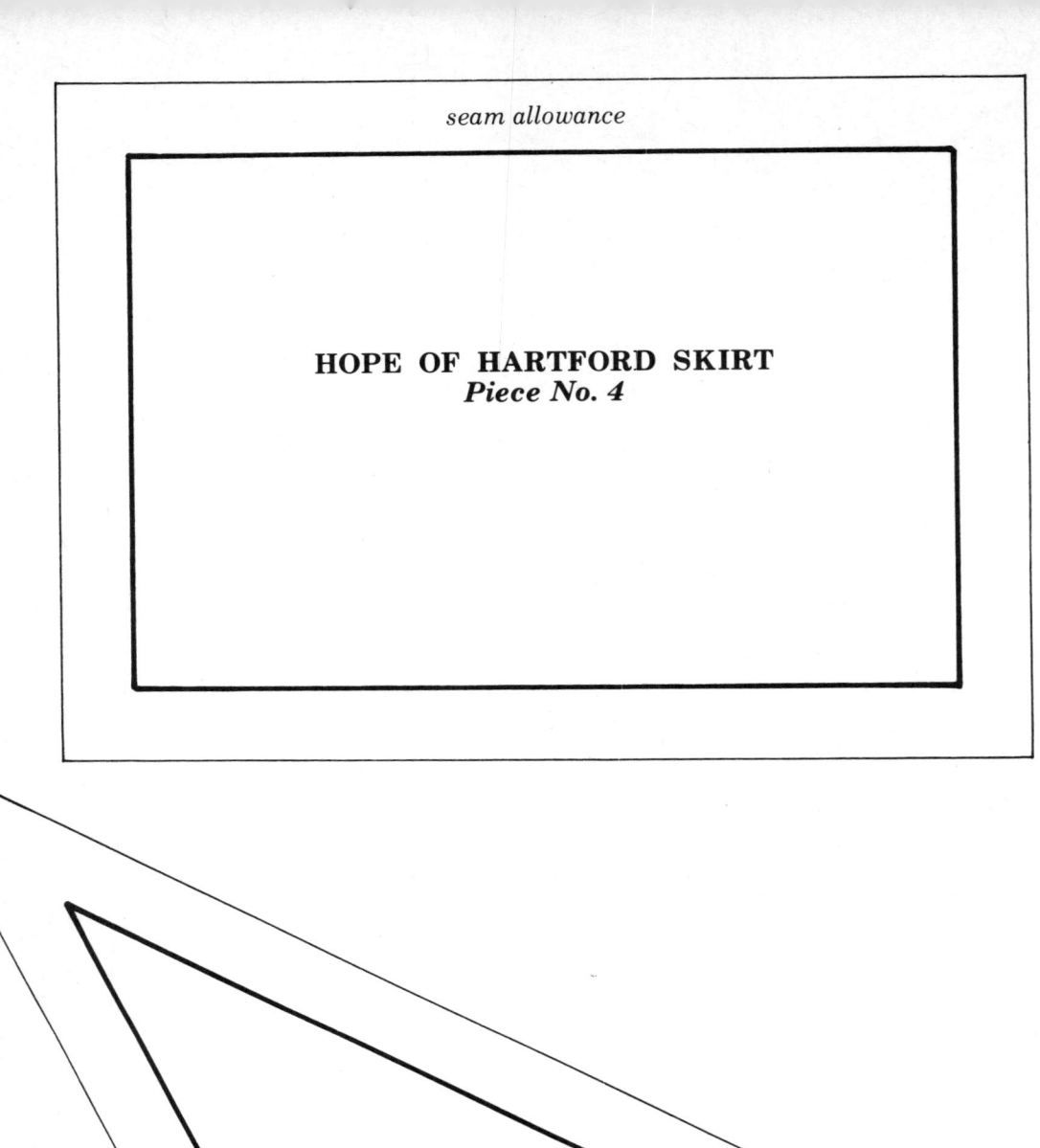

SPIDER WEB SKIRT
Piece No. 1

seam allowance

PLATE 2

seam allowance

SPIDER WEB SKIRT
Piece No. 2

SPIDER WEB SKIRT
Piece No. 3

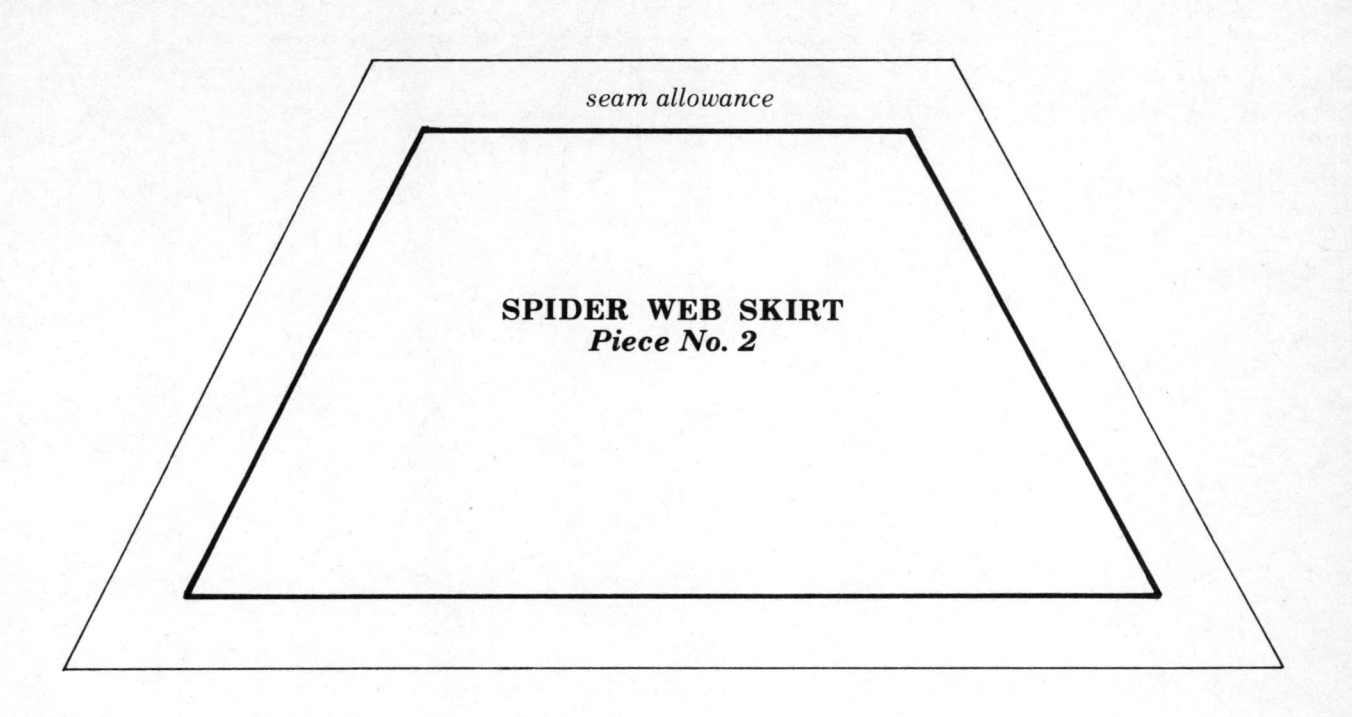

seam allowance

PLATE 3

seam allowance

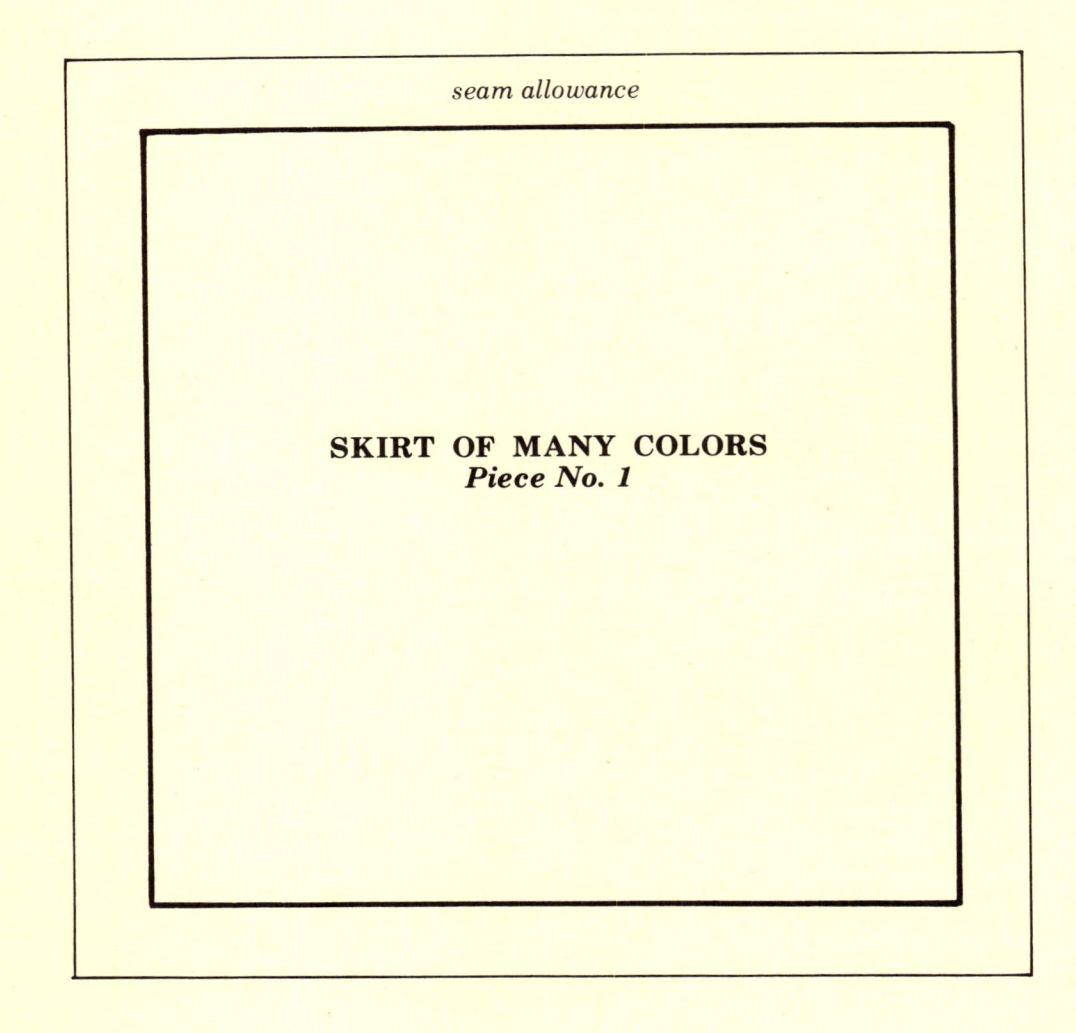

SKIRT OF MANY COLORS
Piece No. 1

PLATE 4

seam allowance

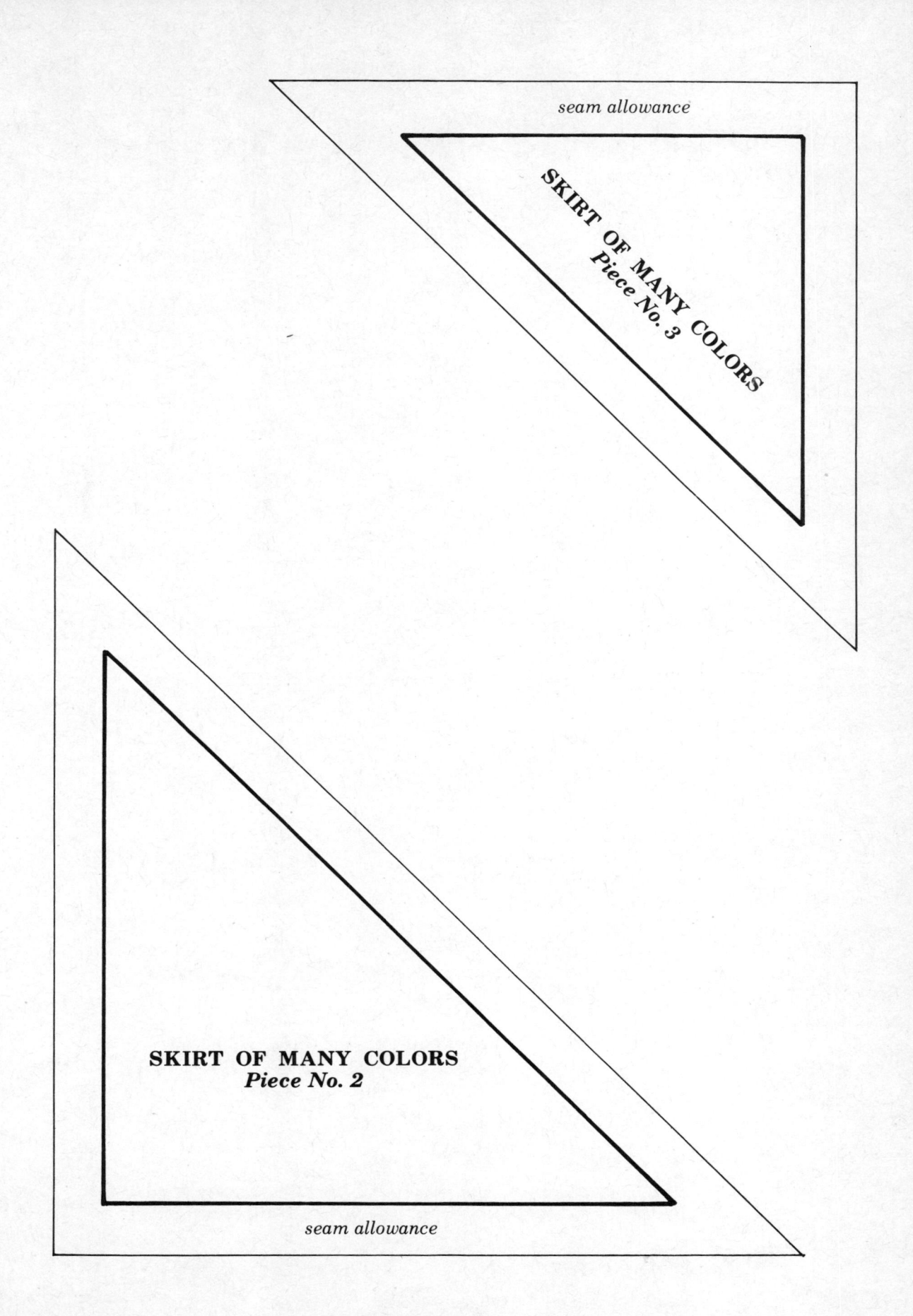

SKIRT OF MANY COLORS
Piece No. 3

SKIRT OF MANY COLORS
Piece No. 2

seam allowance

PLATE 5

seam allowance

HEXAGON SKIRT
Piece No. 1

PLATE 6

HEXAGON SKIRT
Piece No. 2

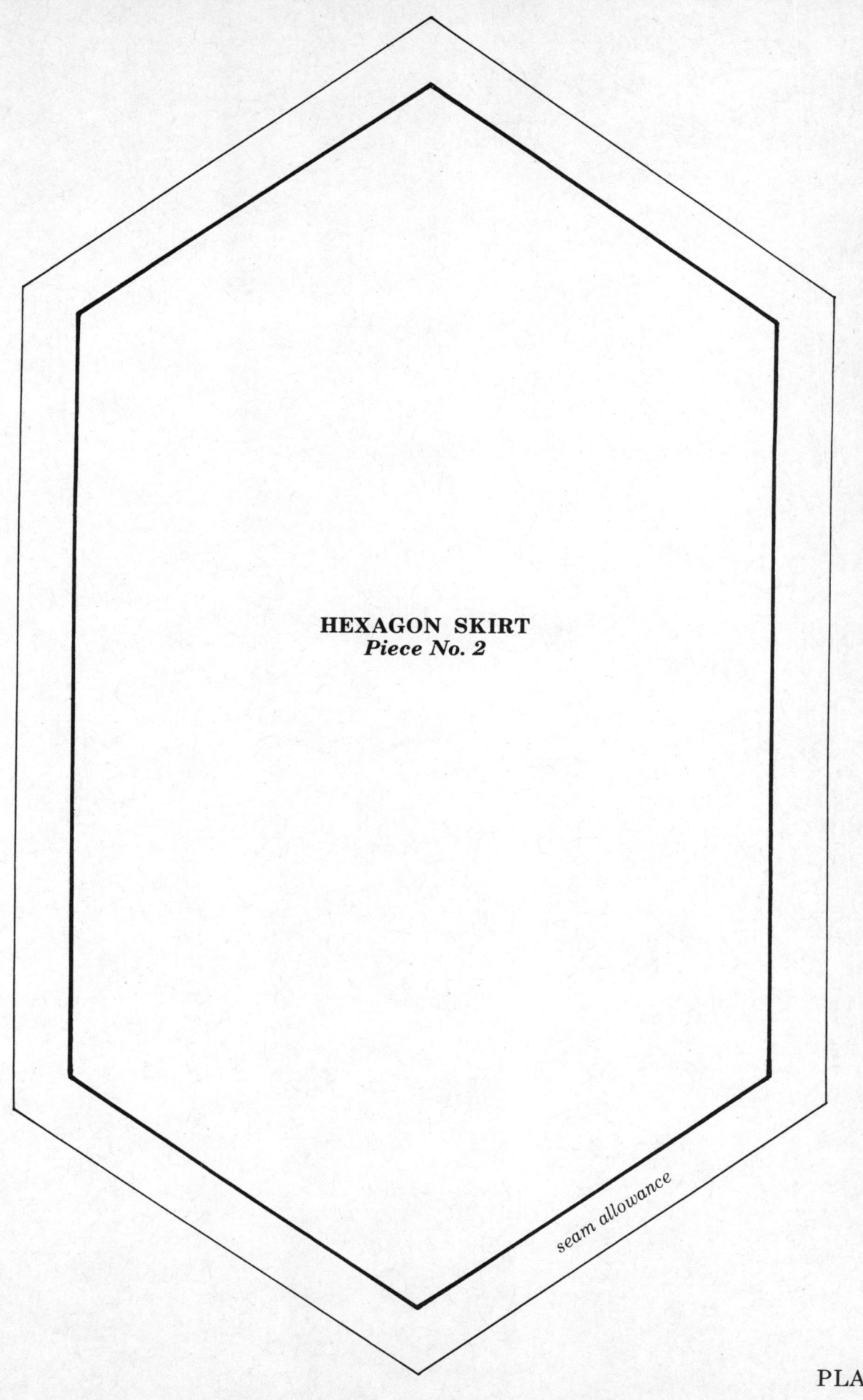

seam allowance

PLATE 7

seam allowance

ONE-PATCH SKIRT
Piece No. 1

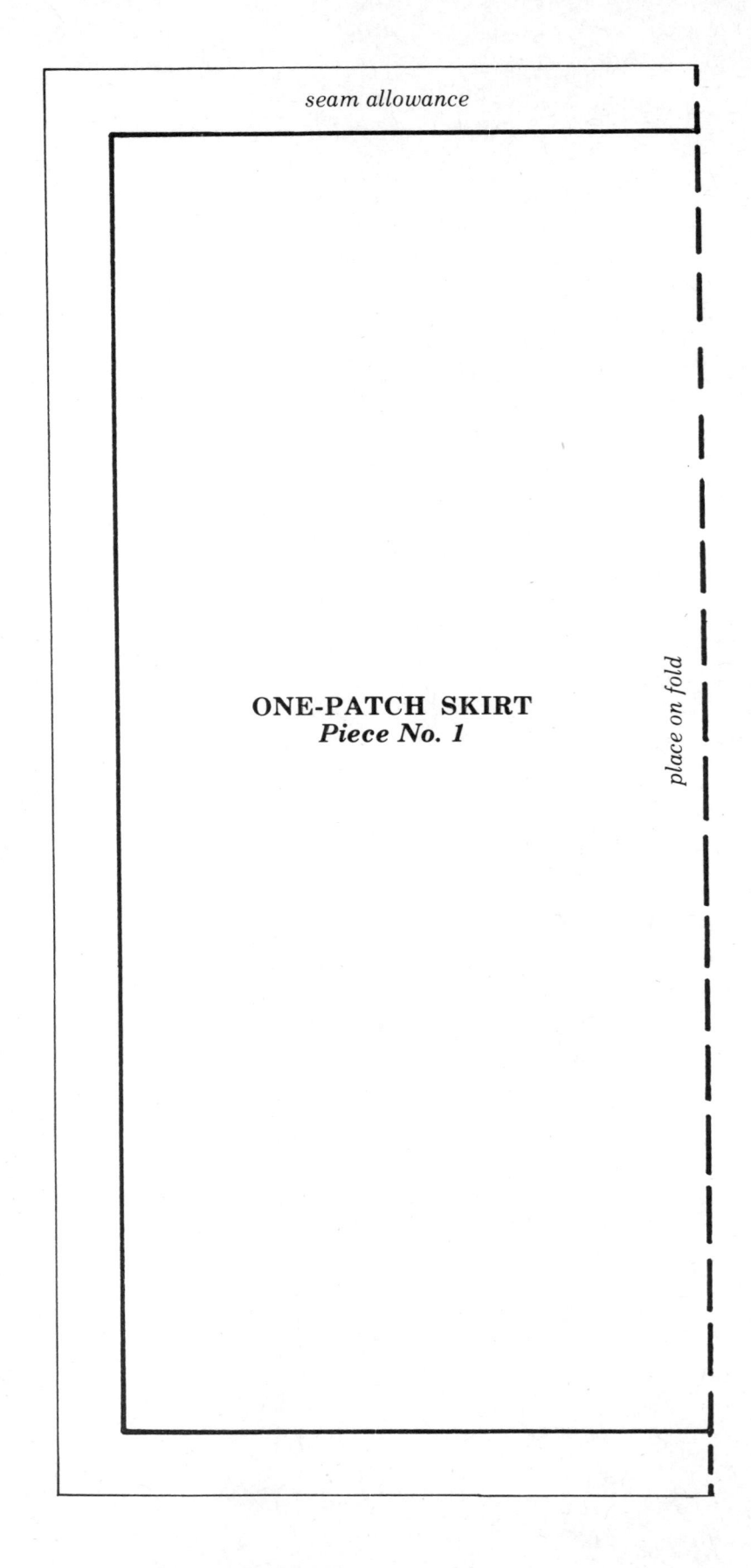

place on fold

PLATE 8

seam allowance

ONE-PATCH SKIRT
Piece No. 2

seam allowance

RAIL FENCE SKIRT
Piece No. 1

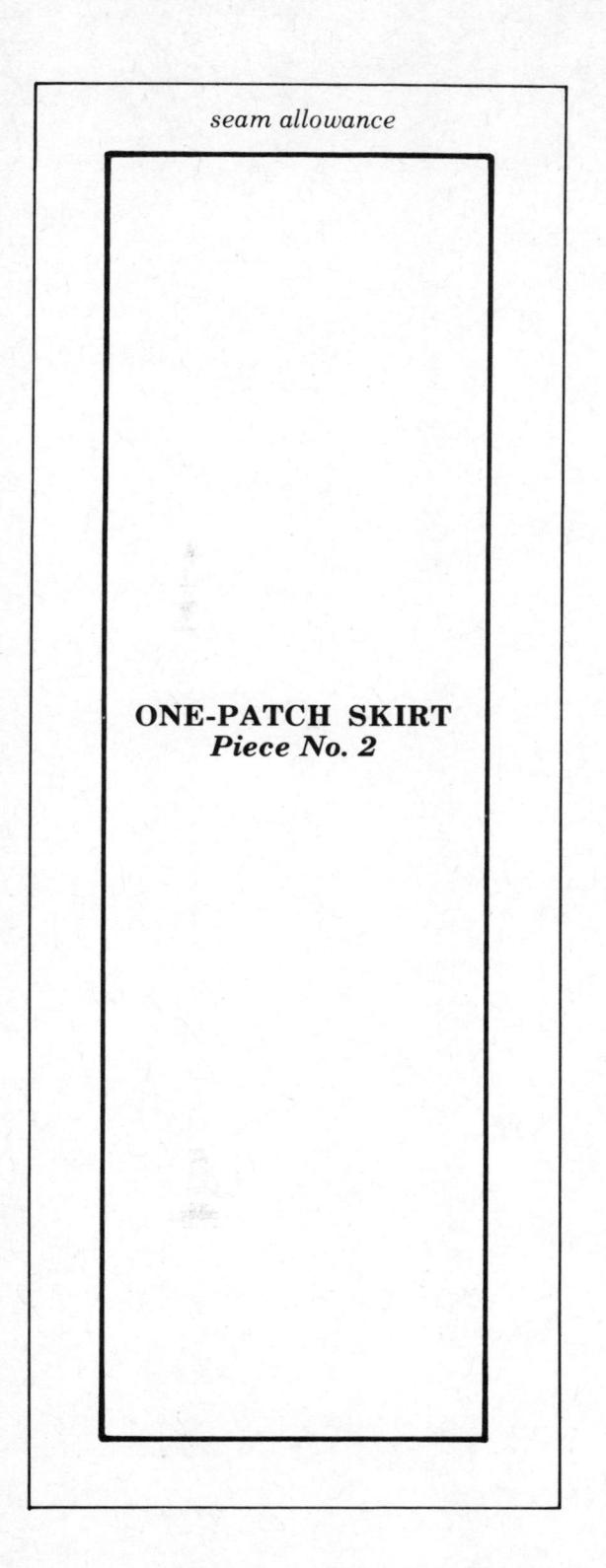

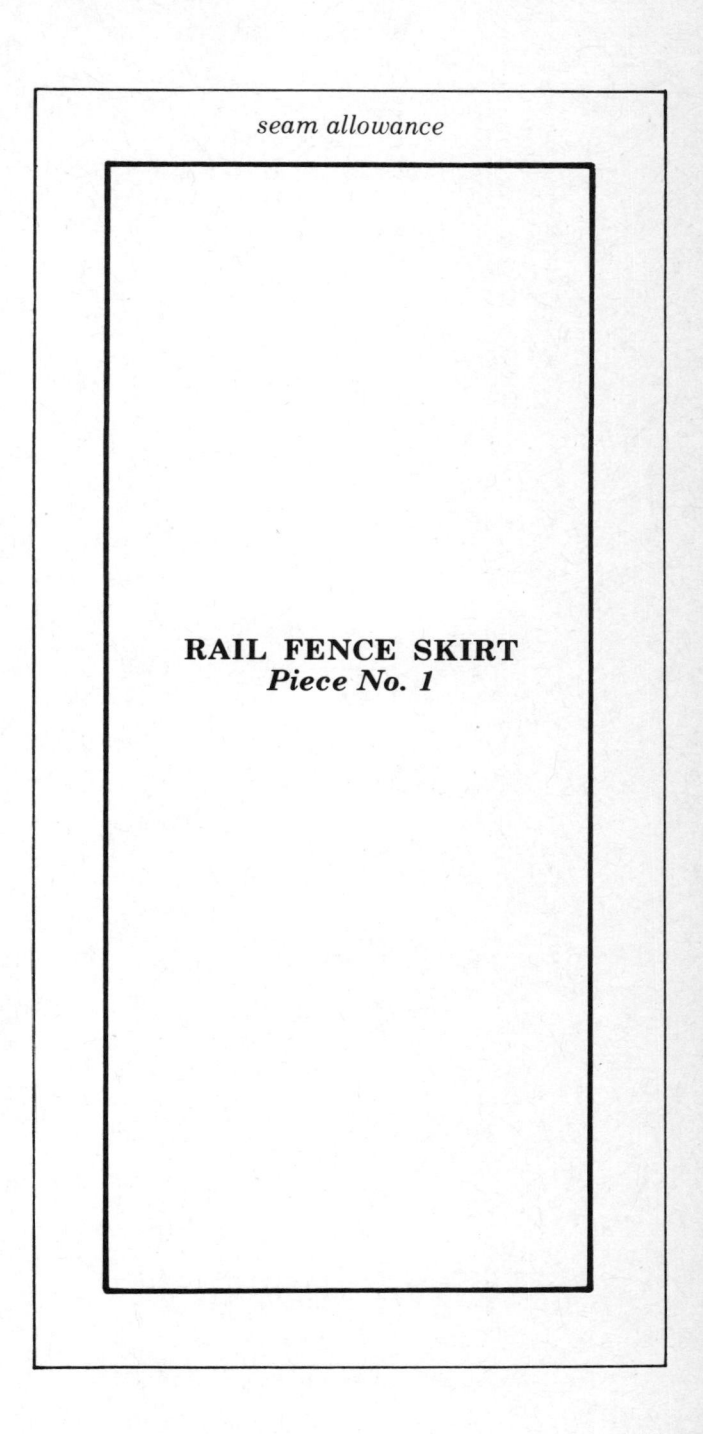

PLATE 9

seam allowance

RAIL FENCE SKIRT
Piece No. 2

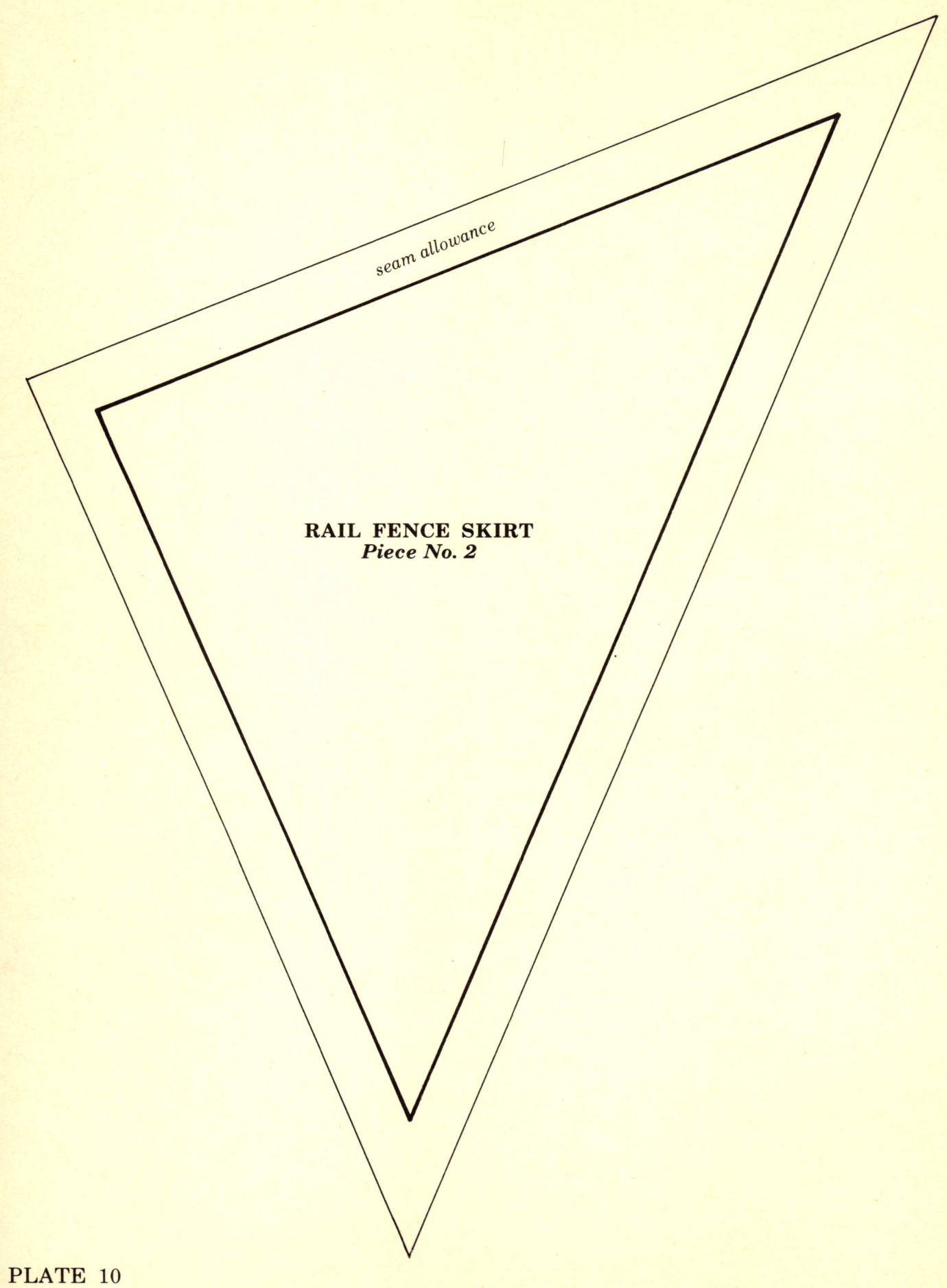

PLATE 10

seam allowance

RAIL FENCE SKIRT
Piece No. 3

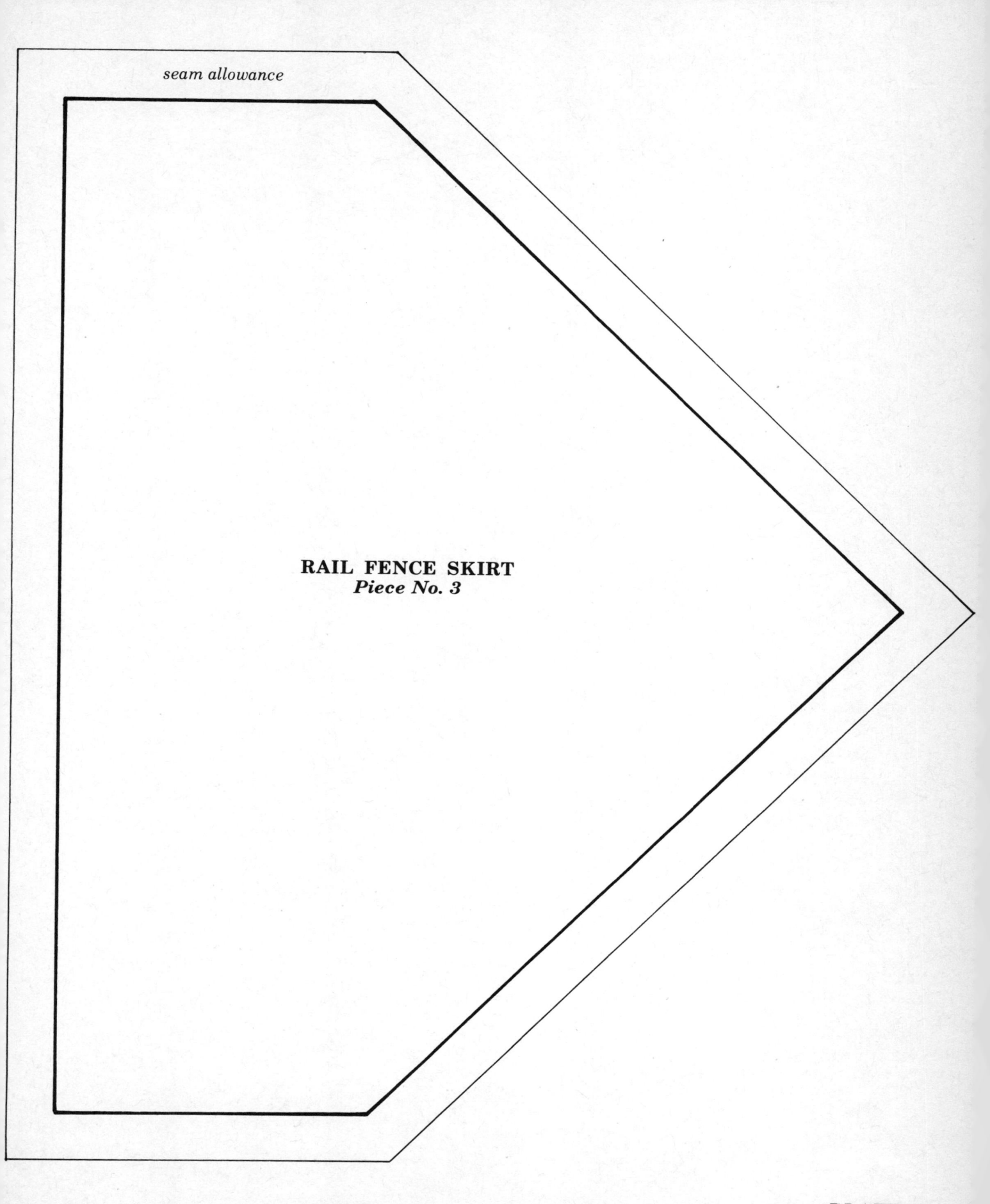

PLATE 11

seam allowance

ROMAN STRIPE SKIRT
Piece No. 2

ROMAN STRIPE SKIRT
Piece No. 3

seam allowance

ROMAN STRIPE SKIRT
Piece No. 4

seam allowance

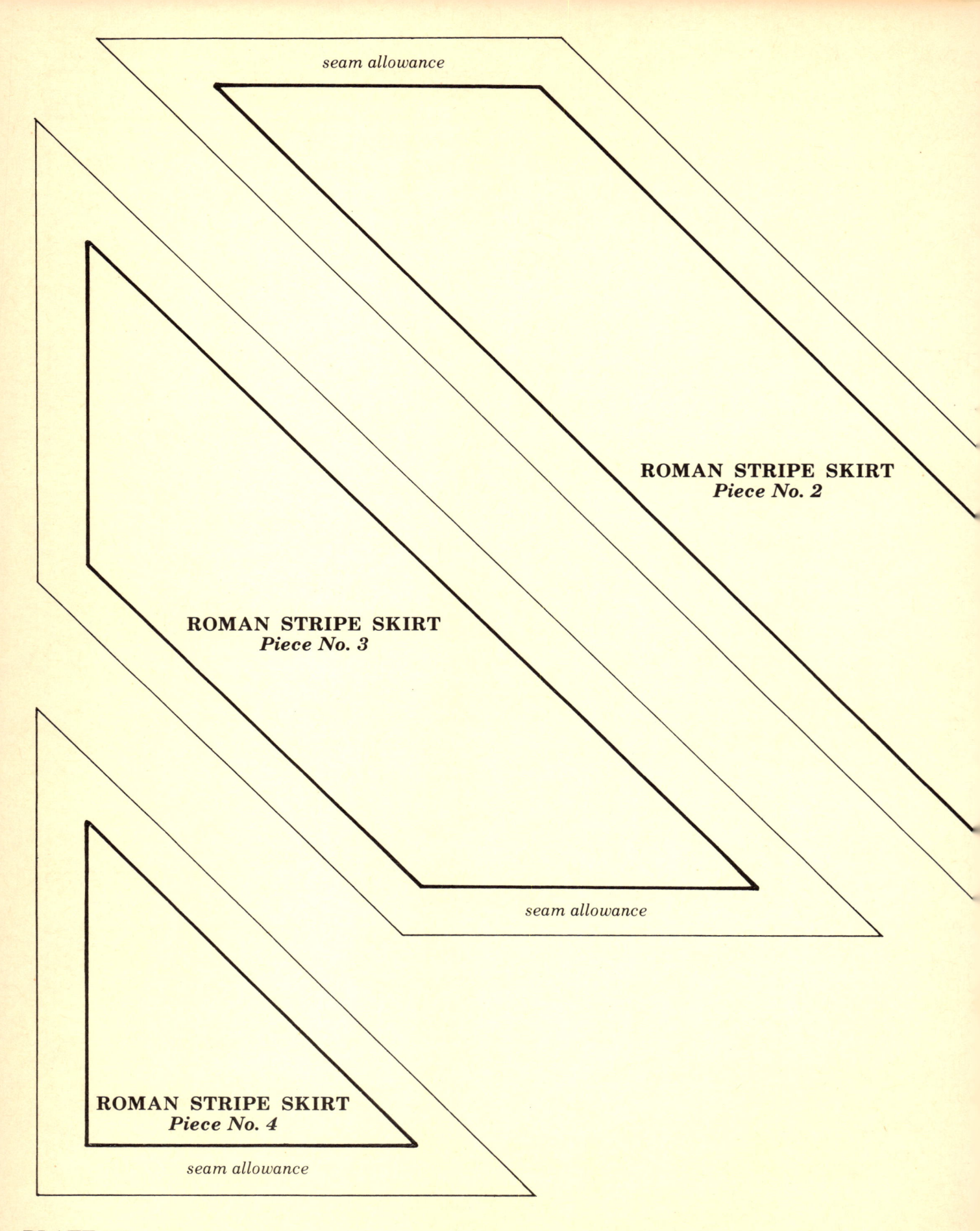

PLATE 12

seam allowance

ROMAN STRIPE SKIRT
Piece No. 1

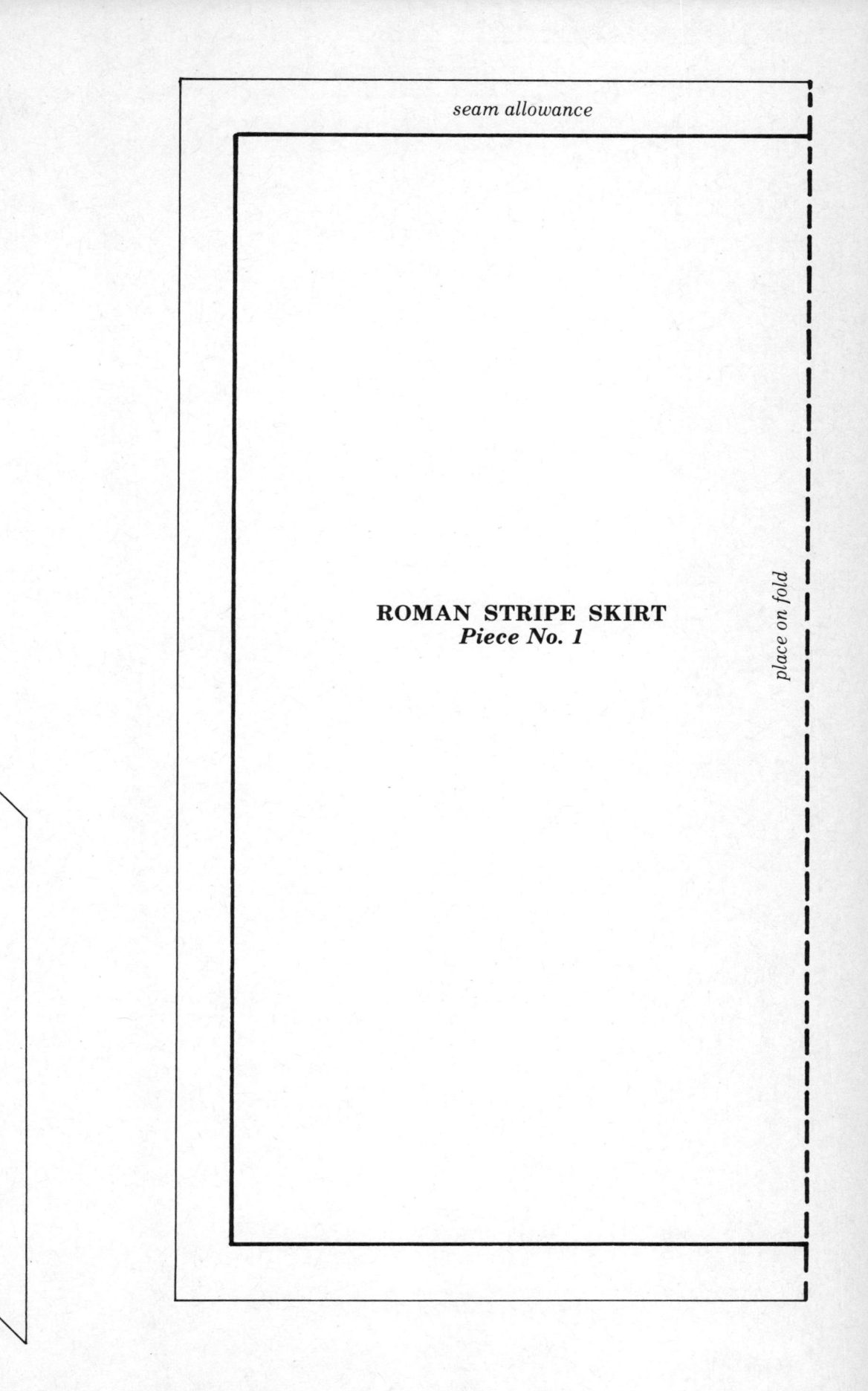

place on fold

PLATE 13

seam allowance

MONKEY WRENCH APRON
Piece No. 1

seam allowance

MONKEY WRENCH APRON
Piece No. 3

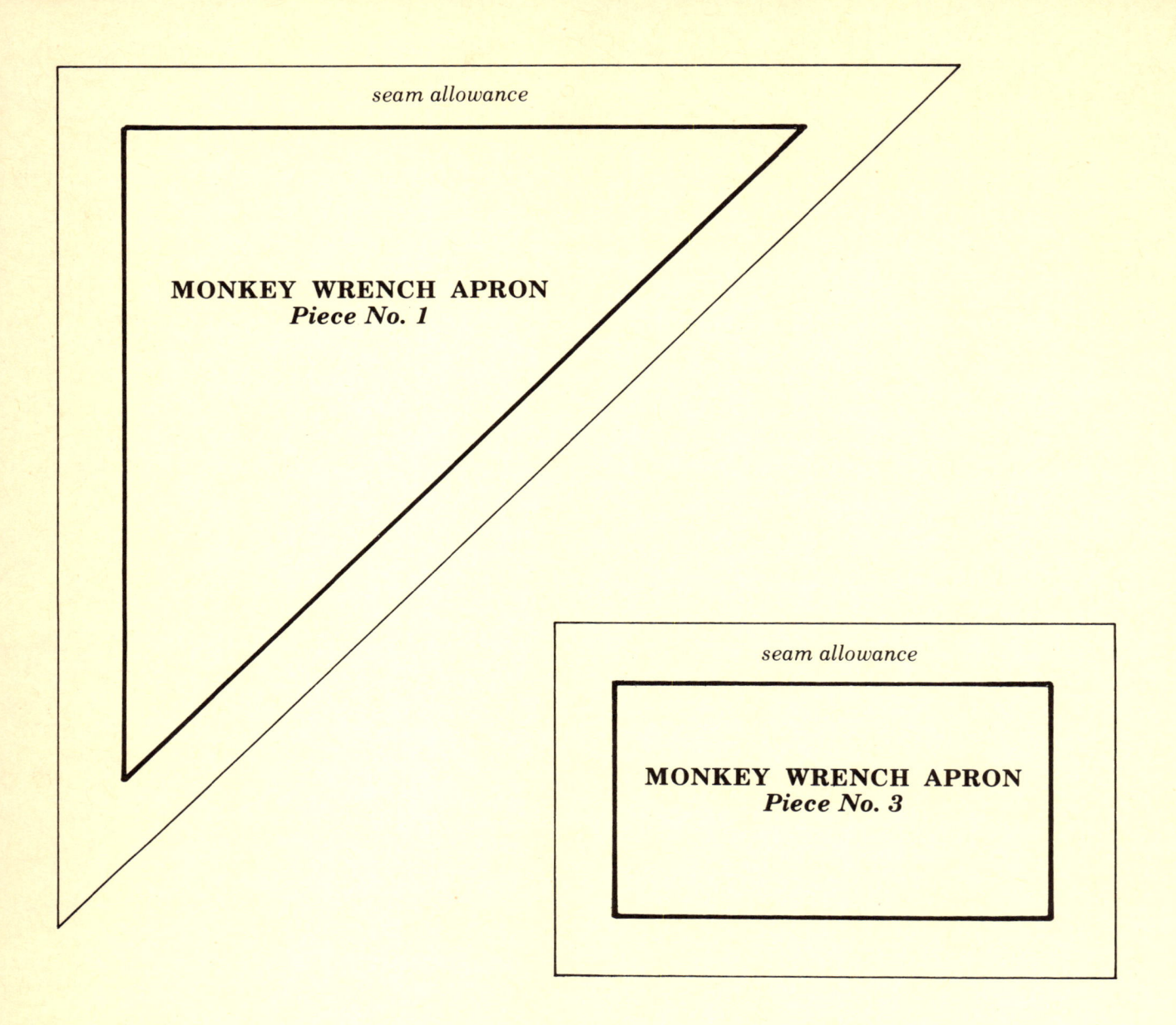

seam allowance

MONKEY WRENCH APRON
Piece No. 2

PLATE 14

seam allowance

MILKY WAY SKIRT
Piece No. 1

PLATE 15

seam allowance

MILKY WAY SKIRT
Piece No. 2

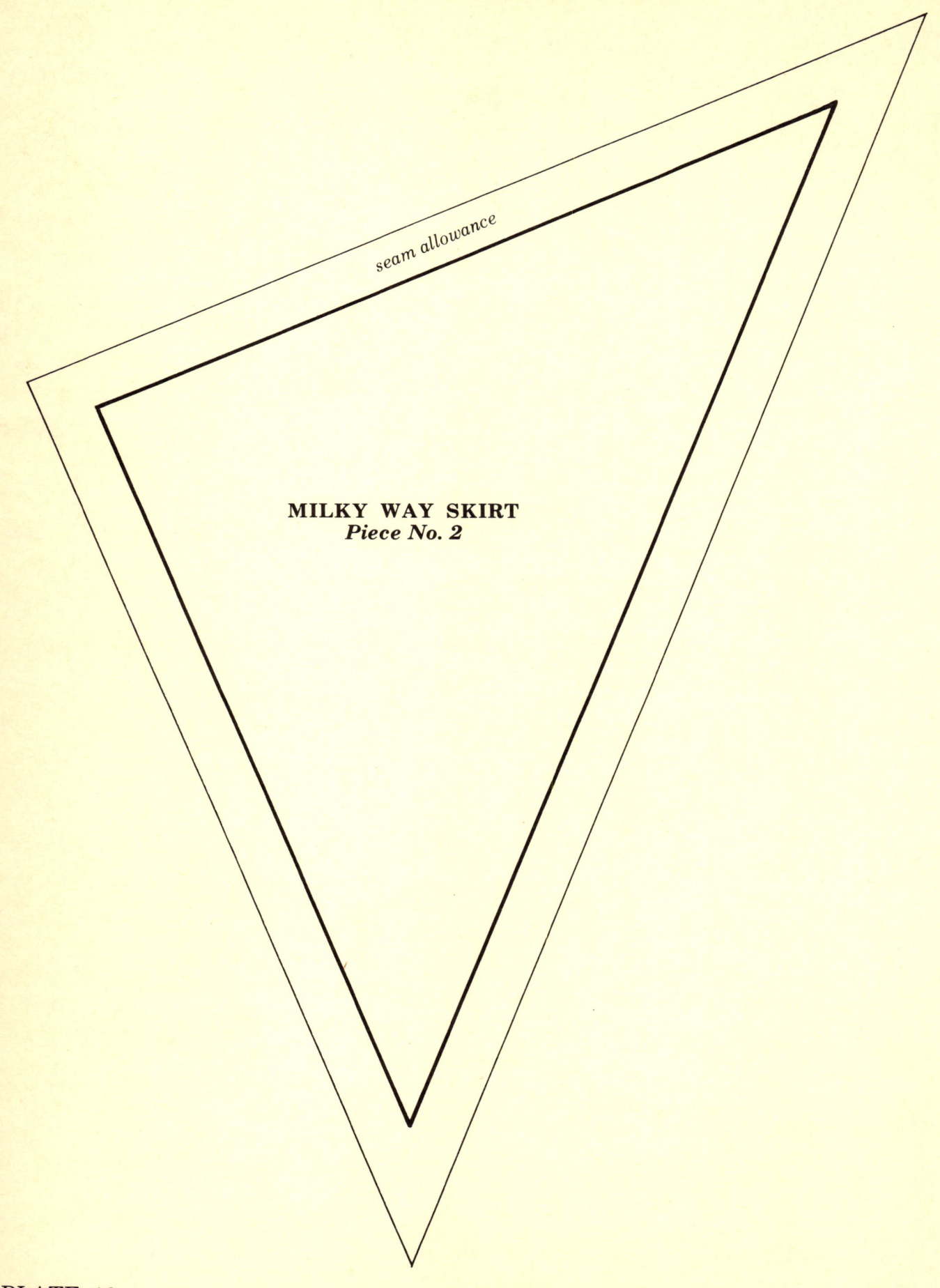

PLATE 16

FOUR-PATCH SKIRT
Piece No. 1

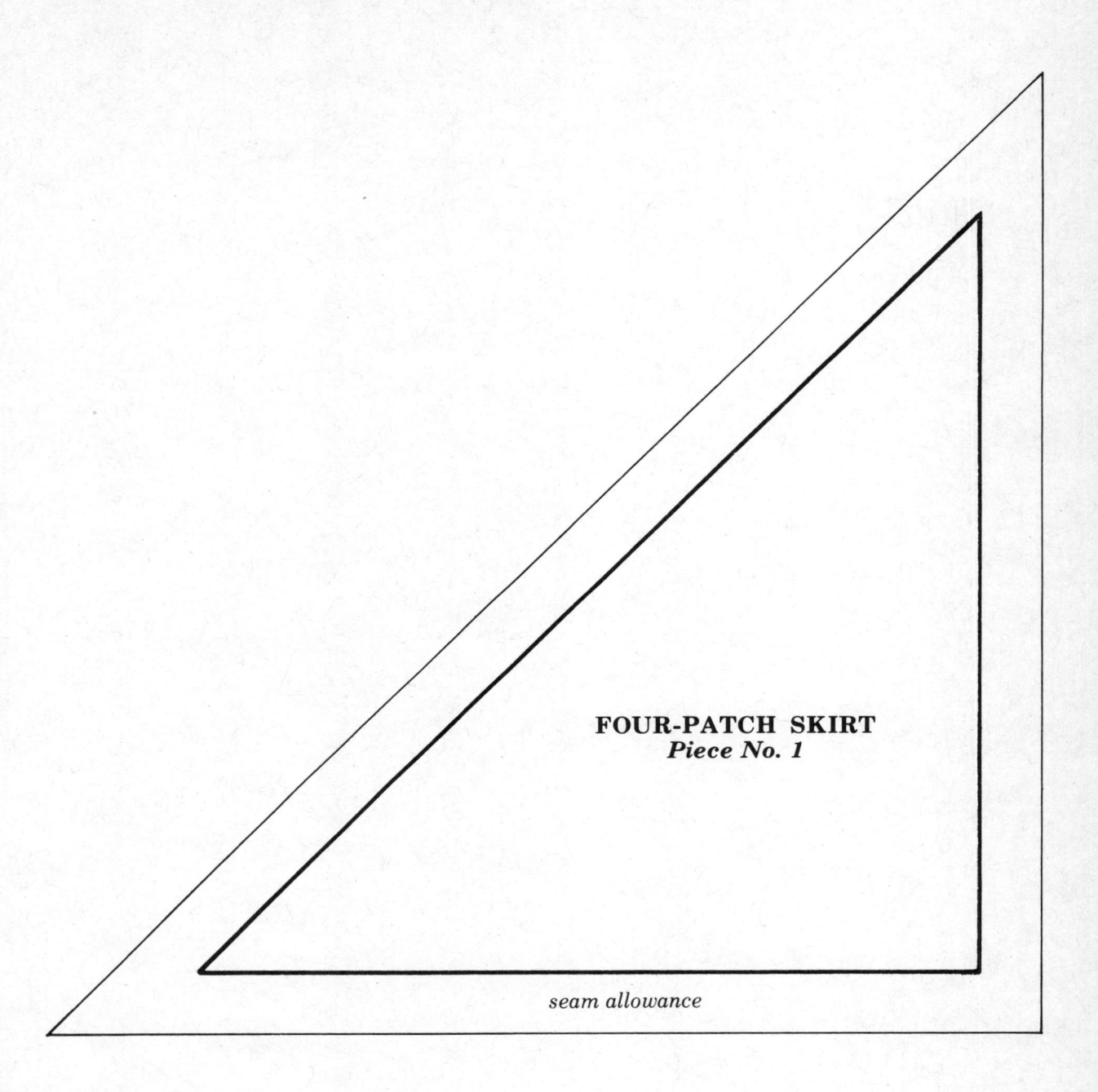

seam allowance

PLATE 17

seam allowance

FOUR-PATCH SKIRT
Piece No. 2

place on fold

PLATE 18

seam allowance

SQUARES AND TRIANGLES SKIRT
Piece No. 1

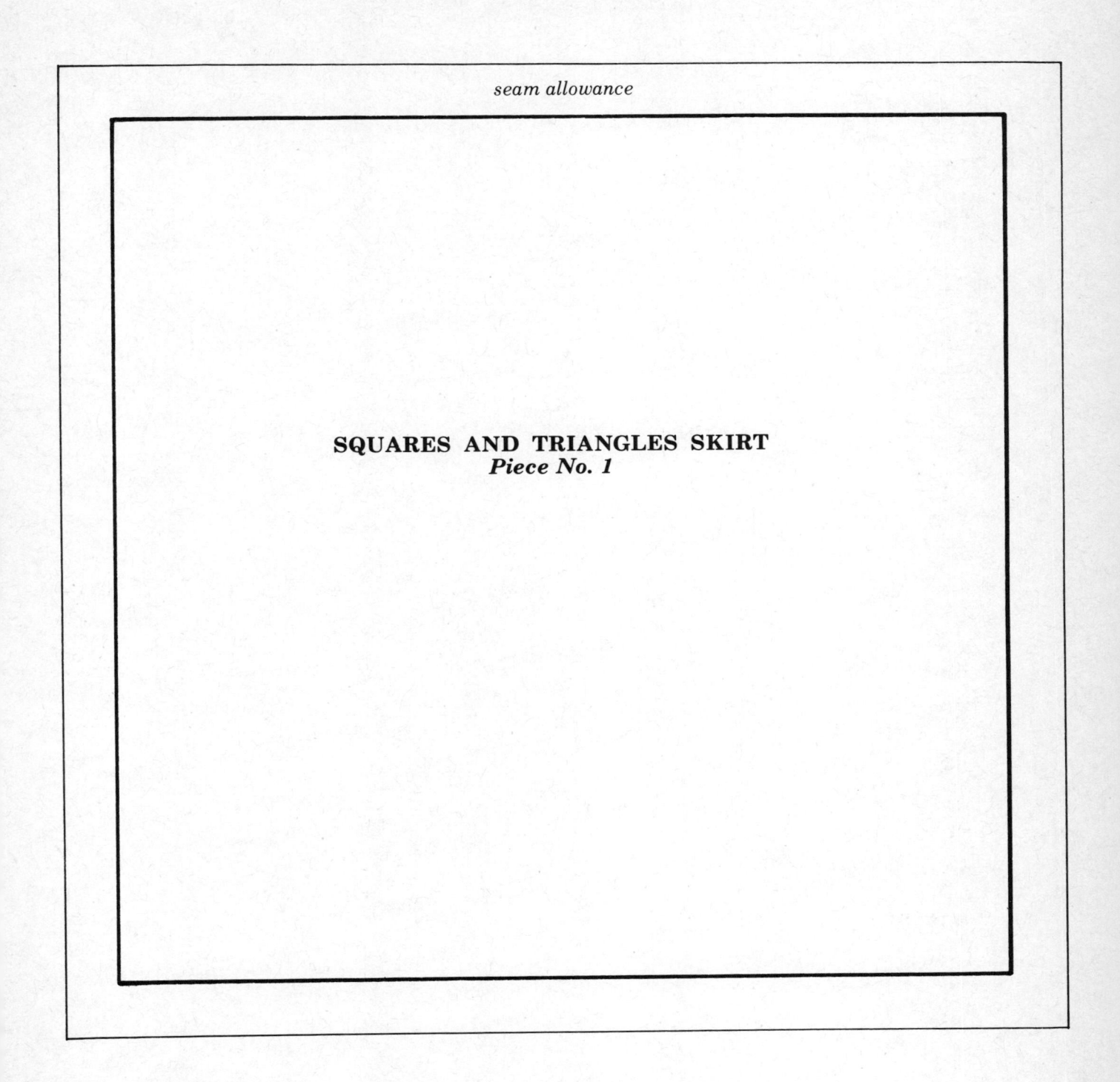

PLATE 19

seam allowance

SQUARES AND TRIANGLES SKIRT
Piece No. 3

SQUARES AND TRIANGLES SKIRT
Piece No. 2

seam allowance

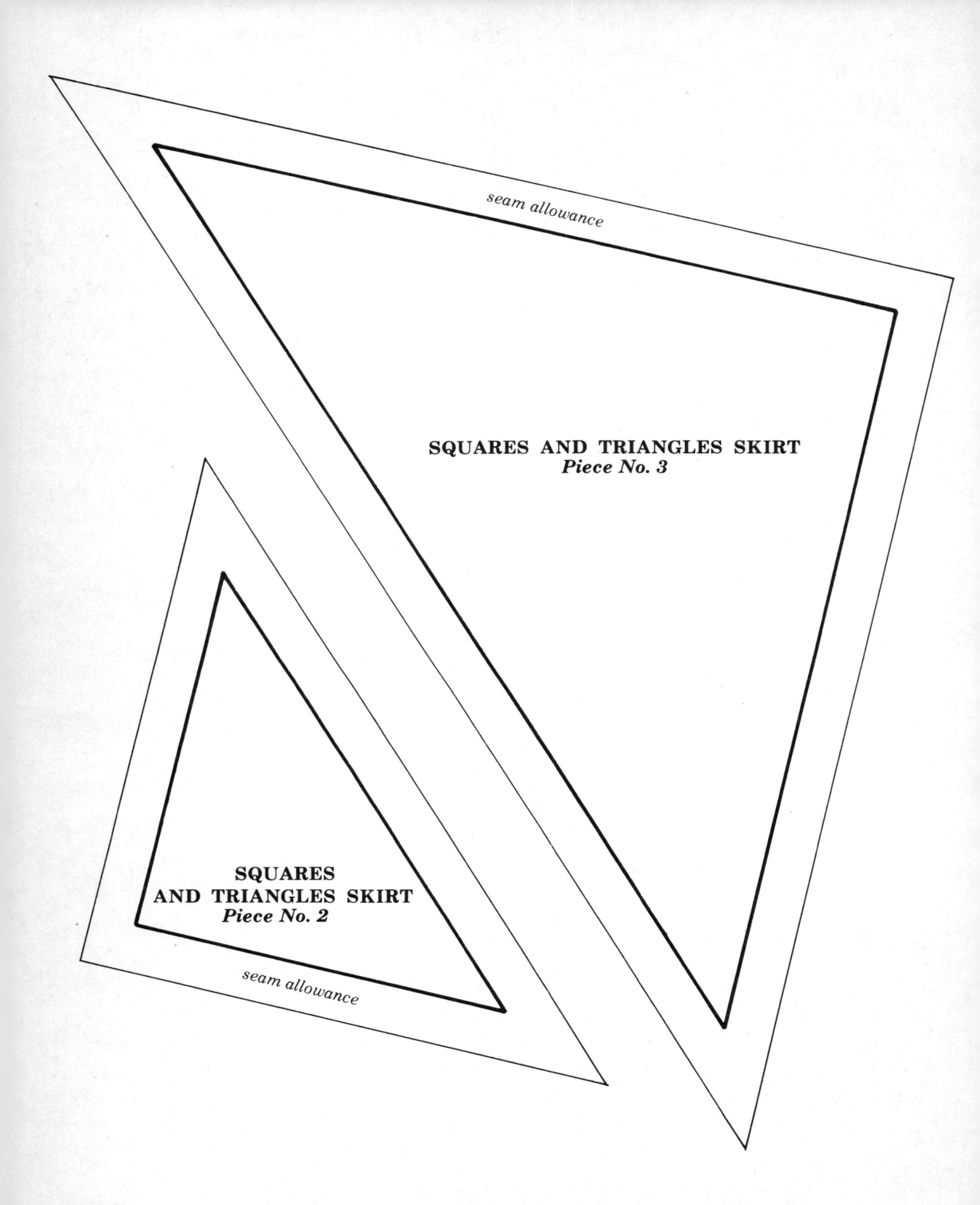

PLATE 20

seam allowance

BROKEN DISHES SKIRT
Piece No. 1

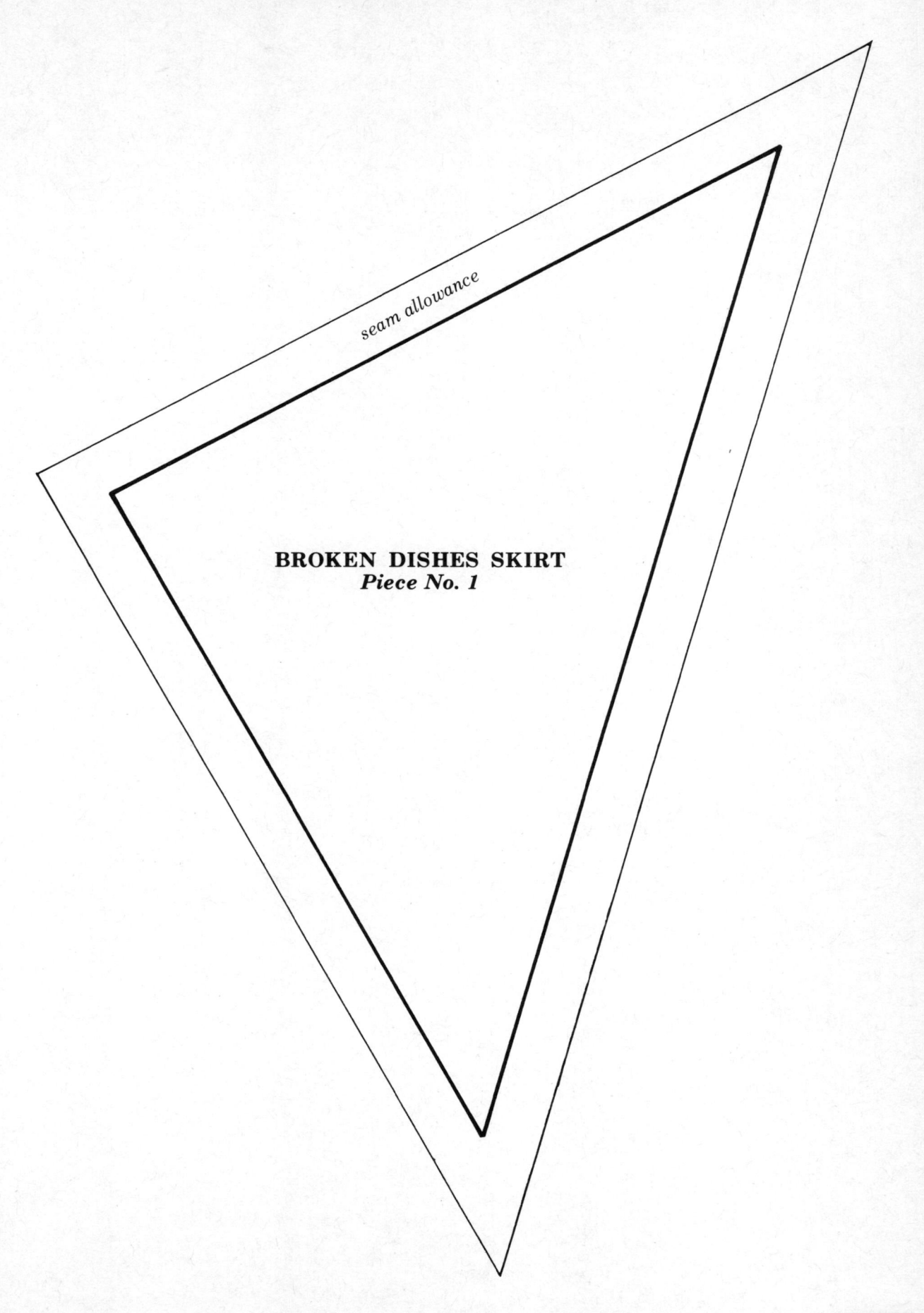

PLATE 21

seam allowance

HIDDEN POCKETS APRON
Piece No. 1

PLATE 22

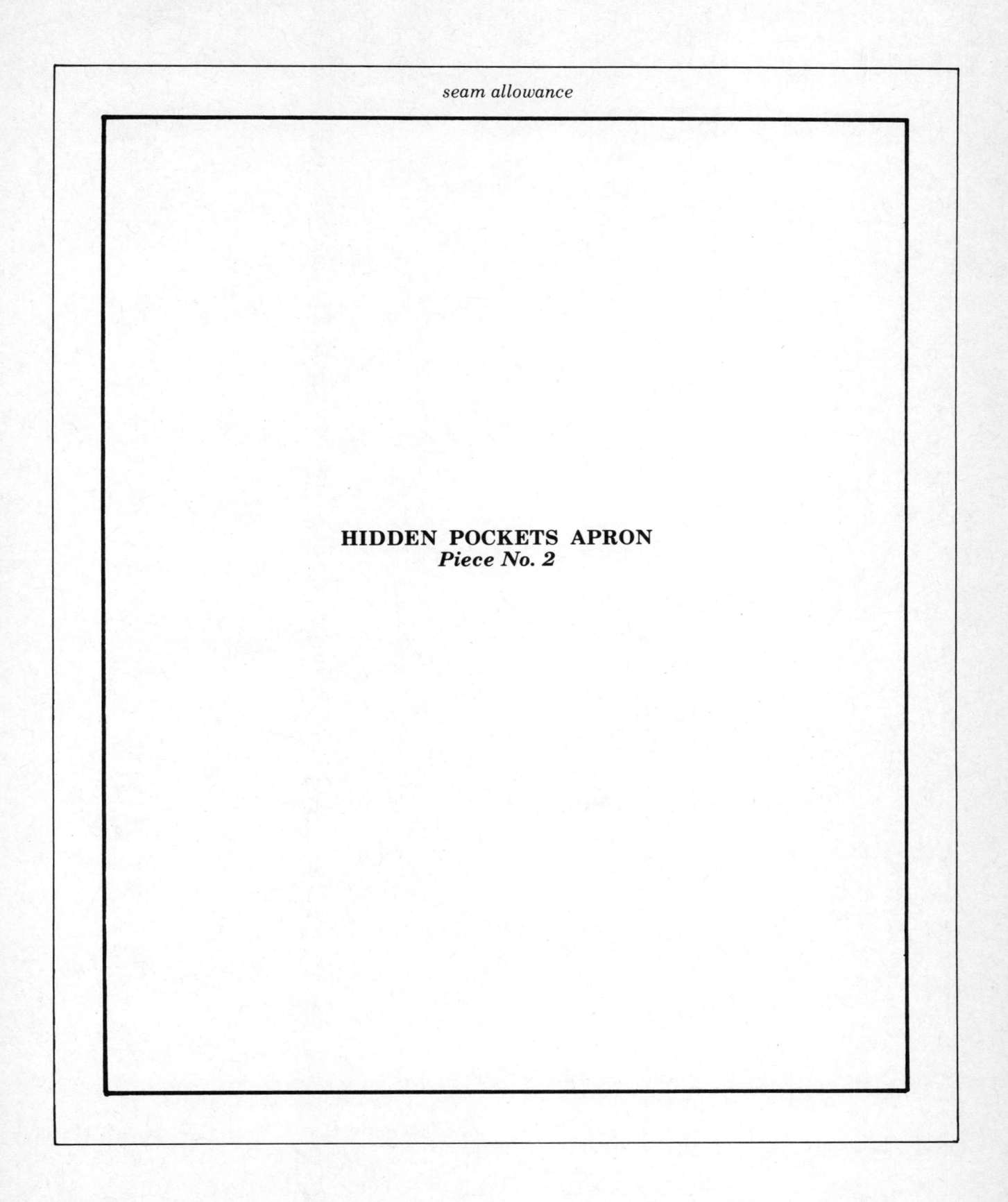

seam allowance

HIDDEN POCKETS APRON
Piece No. 2

PLATE 23

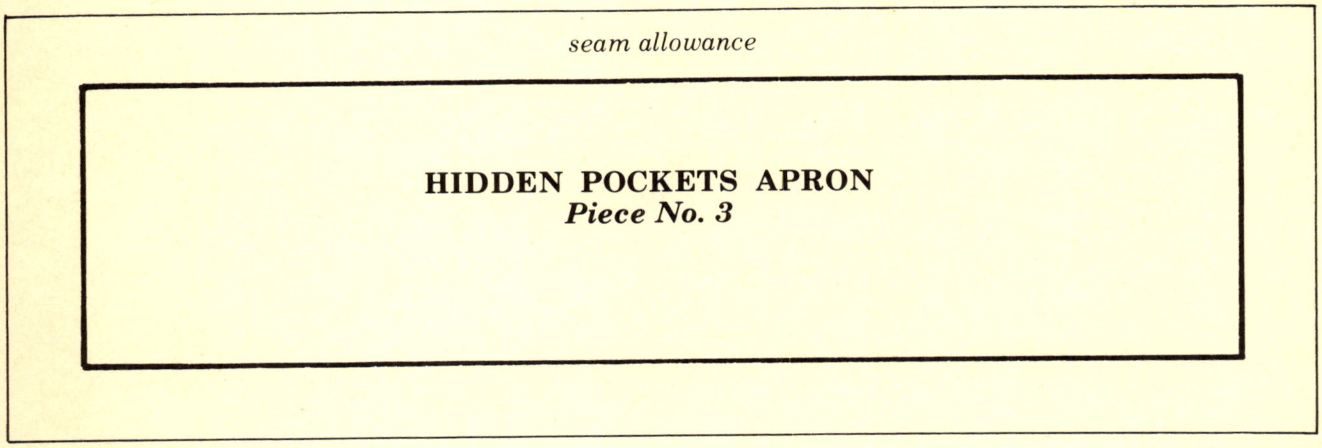

seam allowance

HIDDEN POCKETS APRON
Piece No. 3

PLATE 24

Hidden Pockets Apron

MATERIALS AND EQUIPMENT

Apron fabric: 1 yard green print; 1/2 yard orange; 3/4 yard orange dotted; 3/8 yard yellow print.
Sharp scissors, pencils, straight pins, needles, sewing thread.

DIRECTIONS

Before beginning the apron, read the general directions on pages iii to v.
1. Cut out the appropriate templates on plates 22, 23 and 24.
2. Cut out the required pieces listed below.
3. Hem the pockets made from Piece No. 2. Lay the pockets on the top of two pieces of the same color made from Piece No. 1 and sew both pieces along the sides to the other pieces made from Piece No. 1.
4. Following the apron diagram, assemble the apron. When sewing the row of blocks made from Piece No. 1 to the strips, sew the bottom of the pockets, but leave the top of the pockets open.
5. Make a narrow hem on the sides of the apron.
6. Following the directions in the introduction apply the waistband and ties.
7. Make a 1 1/2" hem on the bottom.

NUMBER OF PIECES TO BE CUT

Piece No. 1 .... 2 Green Print
Piece No. 1 .... 2 Orange
Piece No. 2 .... 2 Green Print
Piece No. 3 .... 6 Yellow Print
Piece No. 3 .... 4 Orange Dotted
Strip A (2 3/4" × 30 3/4") .... 1 Green Print
Strip A .... 2 Orange
Strip B (4 1/4" × 30 3/4") .... 1 Green Print
Waistband and Ties (3 3/4" × 70 3/4") .... 1 Green Print

APRON DIAGRAM

One-Patch Skirt

MATERIALS AND EQUIPMENT

Skirt fabric: 1 5/8 yards multi-color stripe; 1/4 yard yellow gingham; 1/4 yard red gingham; 1/4 yard green gingham; 7/8 yard green print; 7/8 yard yellow dotted swiss; 7/8 yard pink.
Lining fabric: 1 3/4 yards.
Sharp scissors, pencils, straight pins, needles, zipper or elastic, sewing thread.

DIRECTIONS

Before beginning the skirt, read the general directions on pages iii to v.
1. Cut out the appropriate templates on plates 8 and 9.
2. Cut out the required pieces listed below.
3. Following the skirt diagram, assemble the skirt.
4. Measure the completed skirt and cut the lining material to match.
5. Sew the sides of the skirt together, and sew the sides of the lining together. If you are planning to use a zipper in the skirt, be sure to leave the appropriate opening at the top.
6. Lay the wrong side of the lining on the wrong side of the skirt with the top edges of the skirt and lining even. Sew the skirt and lining together 1/4" from this top edge.
7. Following the directions in the introduction, apply either the elastic casing or the waistband to the skirt.
8. Hem the skirt and the lining separately.

NUMBER OF PIECES TO BE CUT

Piece No. 1 ....18 Striped
Piece No. 2 ....6 Yellow Gingham
Piece No. 2 ....6 Red Gingham
Piece No. 3 ....6 Green Gingham
Strip A (2 3/4" × 54 3/4") ....2 Green Print
Strip A (2 3/4" × 54 3/4") ....2 Yellow Dotted Swiss
Strip A (2 3/4" × 54 3/4") ....1 Pink
Strip B (54 3/4" × sufficient width to give
   desired length to skirt plus 3 1/4" for the hem) ...1 Pink
Waistband (3 3/4" × the desired length) ....1 Striped
or
Elastic Casing (3 1/4" × 54 3/4") ....1 Striped

	34″	

| Waistband or elastic casing (striped) |
| Strip A (pink) |
| Strip A (yellow dotted swiss) |

8″

| 1 (striped) | 2 (yellow gingham) | 1 (striped) | 2 (red gingham) | 1 (striped) | 2 (green gingham) | 1 (striped) | 2 (yellow gingham) | 1 (striped) | 2 (red gingham) | 1 (striped) | 2 (green gingham) |

| Strip A (green print) |

| 1 (striped) | 2 (red gingham) | 1 (striped) | 2 (green gingham) | 1 (striped) | 2 (yellow gingham) | 1 (striped) | 2 (red gingham) | 1 (striped) | 2 (green gingham) | 1 (striped) | 2 (yellow gingham) |

| Strip A (green print) |

| 1 (striped) | 2 (green gingham) | 1 (striped) | 2 (yellow gingham) | 1 (striped) | 2 (red gingham) | 1 (striped) | 2 (green gingham) | 1 (striped) | 2 (yellow gingham) | 1 (striped) | 2 (red gingham) |

| Strip A (yellow dotted swiss) |
| Strip B (pink) |

54″

Rail Fence Skirt

MATERIALS AND EQUIPMENT

Skirt fabric: 1/2 yard blue check; 1/2 yard blue print; 3/8 yard yellow print; 3/8 yard yellow check; 3/8 yard red print; 3/8 yard red and blue print; 3/8 yard red dotted; 1/2 yard dark print.
Lining fabric: 1 3/4 yards.
Sharp scissors, pencils, straight pins, needles, zipper or elastic, sewing thread.

DIRECTIONS

Before beginning the skirt, read the general directions on pages iii to v.

1. Cut out the appropriate templates on plates 9, 10 and 11.
2. Cut out the required pieces listed below.
3. Following the skirt diagram, assemble the skirt.
4. Measure the completed skirt and cut the lining material to match.
5. Sew the sides of the skirt together, and sew the sides of the lining together. If you are planning to use a zipper in the skirt, be sure to leave the appropriate opening at the top.
6. Lay the wrong side of the lining on the wrong side of the skirt with the top edges of the skirt and the lining even. Sew the skirt and lining together 1/4″ from this top edge.
7. Following the directions in the introduction, apply either the elastic casing or the waistband to the skirt.
8. Hem the skirt and the lining separately.

NUMBER OF PIECES TO BE CUT

Piece No. 1 ....21 Blue Check (BC)
Piece No. 1 ....21 Blue Print (BP)
Piece No. 1 ....14 Yellow Print (YP)
Piece No. 1 ....14 Yellow Check (YC)
Piece No. 1 ....14 Red Print (RP)
Piece No. 1 ....14 Red and Blue Print (RBP)
Piece No. 1 ....14 Dark Print (DP)
Piece No. 1 ....14 Red Dotted (RD)
Piece No. 2 ....1 Blue Check (BC)
Piece No. 2 ....1 Blue Print (BP)
Piece No. 2 ....1 Yellow Print (YP)
Piece No. 2 ....1 Yellow Check (YC)
Piece No. 2 ....1 Red Print (RP)
Piece No. 2 ....1 Red and Blue Print (RBP)
Piece No. 2 ....1 Dark Print (DP)
Piece No. 3 ....1 Blue Check (BC)
Piece No. 3 ....1 Blue Print (BP)
Piece No. 3 ....1 Yellow Print (YP)
Piece No. 3 ....1 Yellow Check (YC)
Piece No. 3 ....1 Red Print (RP)
Piece No. 3 ....1 Red and Blue Print (RBP)
Piece No. 3 ....1 Dark Print (DP)
Waistband (3 3/4″ × the desired length) ....1 Dark Print
or
Elastic Casing (3 1/4″ × 55″) ....1 Dark Print

14

← 54 1/4″ →

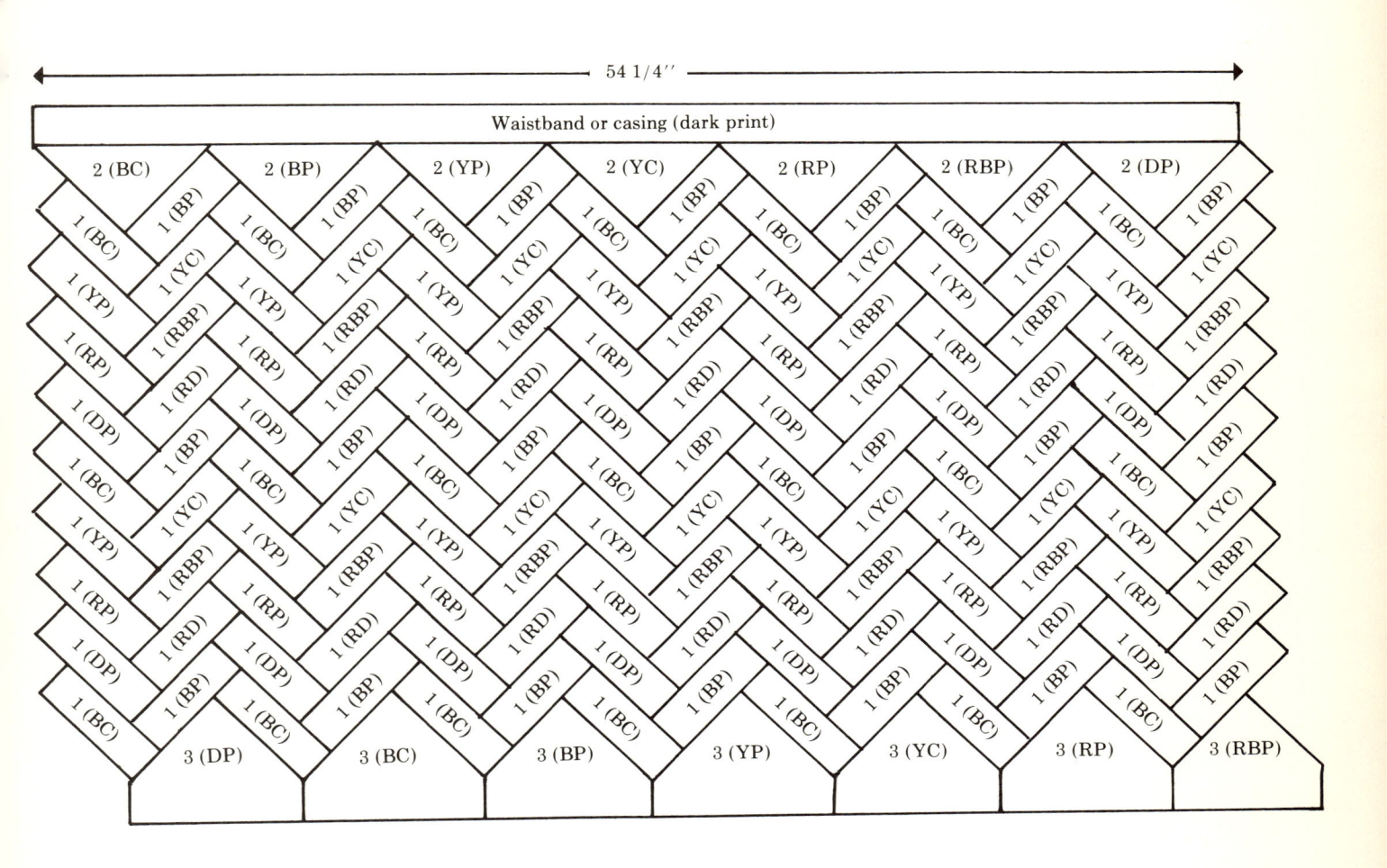

| Waistband or casing (dark print) |

2 (BC) 2 (BP) 2 (YP) 2 (YC) 2 (RP) 2 (RBP) 2 (DP)

3 (DP) 3 (BC) 3 (BP) 3 (YP) 3 (YC) 3 (RP) 3 (RBP)

15

Roman Stripe Skirt

MATERIALS AND EQUIPMENT

Skirt fabric: 1 1/2 yards blue; 1 1/2 yards of various prints.
Lining fabric: 1 7/8 yards.
Sharp scissors, pencils, straight pins, needles, zipper, sewing thread.

DIRECTIONS

Before beginning the skirt, read the general directions on pages iii to v.
1. Cut out the appropriate templates on plates 12 and 13.
2. Cut out the required pieces listed below. Pieces 2, 3 and 4 may be cut from print fabric scraps, using different scraps for each block.
3. Following the block diagram, sew the pieces into 20 pieced blocks.
4. Following the skirt diagram, assemble the pieced blocks and the plain blocks made from Piece No. 1.
5. Measure the completed skirt and cut the lining material to match.
6. Sew the sides of the skirt together, and sew the sides of the lining together. Be sure to leave the appropriate opening at the top for the zipper.
7. Lay the wrong side of the lining on the wrong side of the skirt with the top edges of the skirt and lining even. Sew the skirt and lining together 1/4" from this top edge.
8. Following the directions in the introduction, apply the waistband to the skirt.
9. Hem the skirt and the lining separately.

Note: Another row of blocks can be added to the bottom to make the skirt longer. The bottom row of blocks will be turned under to make a hem; therefore, it will not appear as a full size row of blocks on the right side of the skirt.

NUMBER OF PIECES TO BE CUT

Piece No. 1 ....20 Blue
Piece No. 2 ....40 Print
Piece No. 3 ....40 Print
Piece No. 4 ....40 Print
Waistband (3 1/4" × the desired length) ....1 Blue

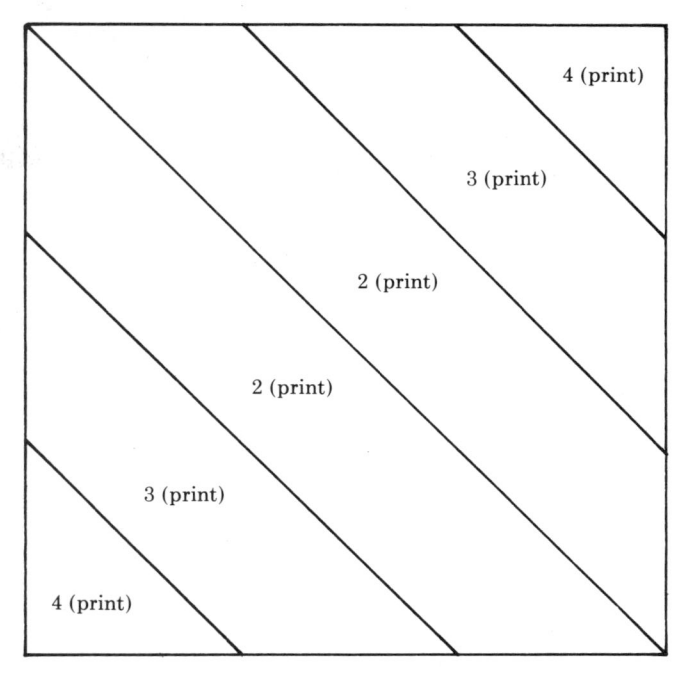

BLOCK DIAGRAM

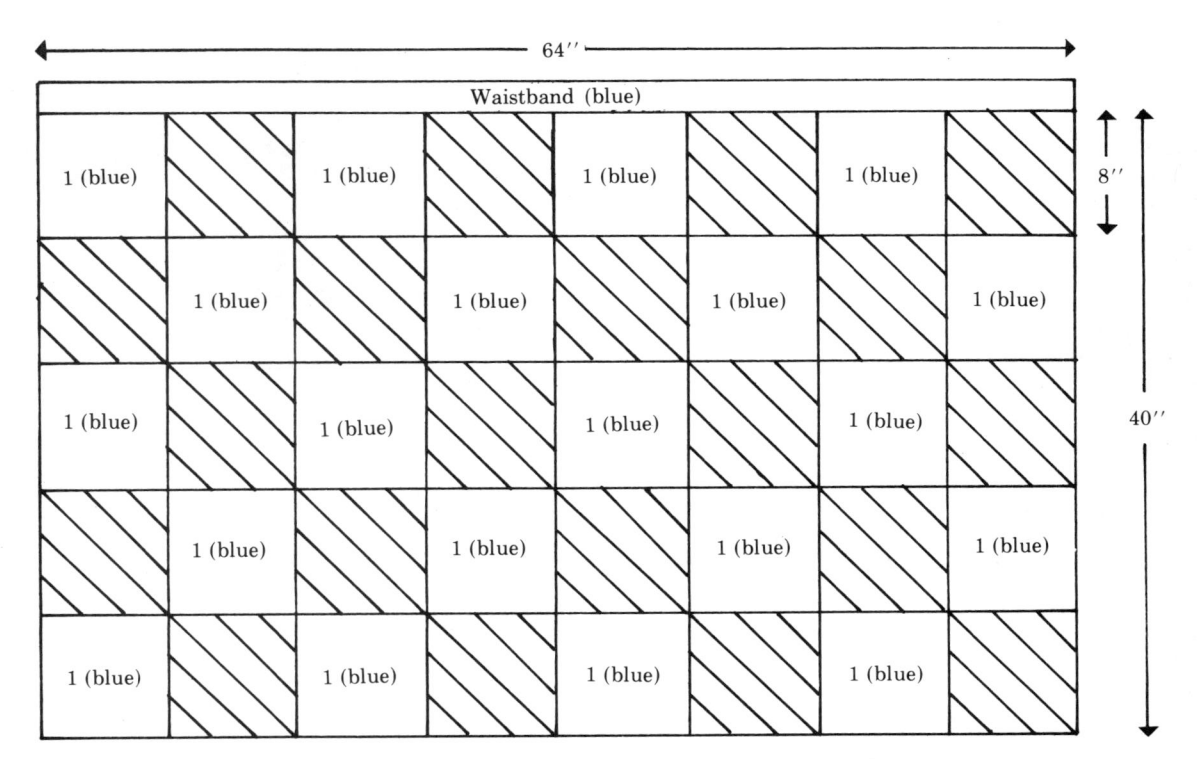

- 4 (print)
- 3 (print)
- 2 (print)
- 2 (print)
- 3 (print)
- 4 (print)

SKIRT DIAGRAM

- 64″
- Waistband (blue)
- 1 (blue)
- 8″
- 40″

17

Milky Way Skirt

MATERIALS AND EQUIPMENT

Skirt fabric: 1 5/8 yards blue; 1/4 yard red calico; 1/4 yard red print; 1/4 yard yellow dotted swiss; 1/4 yard yellow print; 1/4 yard blue gingham; 1/4 yard blue print; 1/4 yard orange gingham; 1/4 yard orange print.
Lining fabric: 1 3/4 yards.
Sharp scissors, pencils, straight pins, needles, elastic, sewing thread.

DIRECTIONS

Before beginning the skirt, read the general directions on pages iii to v.
1. Cut out the appropriate templates on plates 15 and 16.
2. Cut out the required pieces listed below.
3. Following the skirt diagram, assemble the skirt.
4. Measure the completed skirt and cut the lining material to match.
5. Sew the sides of the skirt together, and sew the sides of the lining together.
6. Lay the wrong side of the lining on the wrong side of the skirt with the top edges of the skirt and lining even. Sew the skirt and lining together 1/4″ from this top edge.
7. Following the directions in the introduction, apply the elastic casing to the skirt.
8. Hem the skirt and lining separately.
Note: Another row of blocks can be added to the bottom to make the skirt longer. The bottom row of blocks will be turned under to make a hem; therefore, it will not appear as a full row of blocks on the right side of the skirt.

NUMBER OF PIECES TO BE CUT

Piece No. 1 ....35 Blue (B)
Piece No. 2 ....8 Red Calico (RC)
Piece No. 2 ....8 Red Print (RP)
Piece No. 2 ....8 Yellow Dotted Swiss (YD)
Piece No. 2 ....8 Yellow Print (YP)
Piece No. 2 ....6 Blue Gingham (BG)
Piece No. 2 ....6 Blue Print (BP)
Piece No. 2 ....6 Orange Gingham (OG)
Piece No. 2 ....6 Orange Print (OP)
Elastic Casing (3 1/4″ × 54 3/4″) ....1 Blue

	Elastic casing (blue)								
1 (B)	2 (YD) / 2 (YP)	1 (B)	2 (RC) / 2 (RP)	1 (B)	2 (YD) / 2 (YP)	1 (B)	2 (RC) / 2 (RP)	1 (B)
2 (OG) / 2 (OP)	1 (B)	2 (BG) / 2 (BP)	1 (B)	2 (OG) / 2 (OP)	1 (B)	2 (BG) / 2 (BP)	1 (B)	1 (B)
1 (B)	2 (RC) / 2 (RP)	1 (B)	2 (YD) / 2 (YP)	1 (B)	2 (RC) / 2 (RP)	1 (B)	2 (YD) / 2 (YP)	1 (B)
2 (BG) / 2 (BP)	1 (B)	2 (OG) / 2 (OP)	1 (B)	2 (BG) / 2 (BP)	1 (B)	2 (OG) / 2 (OP)	1 (B)	1 (B)
1 (B)	2 (YD) / 2 (YP)	1 (B)	2 (RC) / 2 (RP)	1 (B)	2 (YD) / 2 (YP)	1 (B)	2 (RC) / 2 (RP)	1 (B)
2 (OG) / 2 (OP)	1 (B)	2 (BG) / 2 (BP)	1 (B)	2 (OG) / 2 (OP)	1 (B)	2 (BG) / 2 (BP)	1 (B)	1 (B)
1 (B)	2 (RC) / 2 (RP)	1 (B)	2 (YD) / 2 (YP)	1 (B)	2 (RC) / 2 (RP)	1 (B)	2 (YD) / 2 (YP)	1 (B)

54″ × 42″ (front), 6″ squares

Four-Patch Skirt

MATERIALS AND EQUIPMENT

Skirt fabric: 1 yard blue; 1 1/4 yards of various prints; 1 3/4 yards blue dotted swiss.
Lining fabric: 1 3/4 yards.
Sharp scissors, pencils, straight pins, needles, zipper or elastic, sewing thread, 5 yards rick rack (optional).

DIRECTIONS

Before beginning the skirt, read the general directions on pages iii to v.
1. Cut out the appropriate templates on plates 17 and 18.
2. Cut out the required pieces listed below. Piece No. 1 may be cut from print fabric scraps, using different scraps for each block.
3. Following the block diagram, sew the pieces into 16 pieced blocks.
4. Following the skirt diagram, assemble the pieced blocks, the plain blocks made from Piece No. 2 and the strips.
5. Measure the completed skirt and cut the lining material to match.
6. Sew the sides of the skirt together, and sew the sides of the lining together. If you are planning to use a zipper in the skirt, be sure to leave the appropriate opening at the top.
7. Lay the wrong side of the lining on the wrong side of the skirt with the top edges of the skirt and the lining even. Sew the skirt and lining together 1/4″ from this top edge.
8. Following the directions in the introduction, apply either the elastic casing or the waistband to the skirt.
9. Hem skirt and lining separately.
Note: Rick rack can be sewn on the pieces made from Strip A to add decoration to the skirt.

NUMBER OF PIECES TO BE CUT

Piece No. 1 ....64 Print
Piece No. 2 ....16 Blue
Strip A (2 3/4″ × 56 3/4″) ....3 Blue Dotted Swiss
Strip B (56 3/4″ × sufficient width to give desired length plus 3 1/4″ for the hem).....1 Blue Dotted Swiss
Waistband (3 3/4″ × the desired length)
................................1 Blue Dotted Swiss
or
Elastic Casing (3 1/4″ × 56 3/4″) ...1 Blue Dotted Swiss

1 (print)

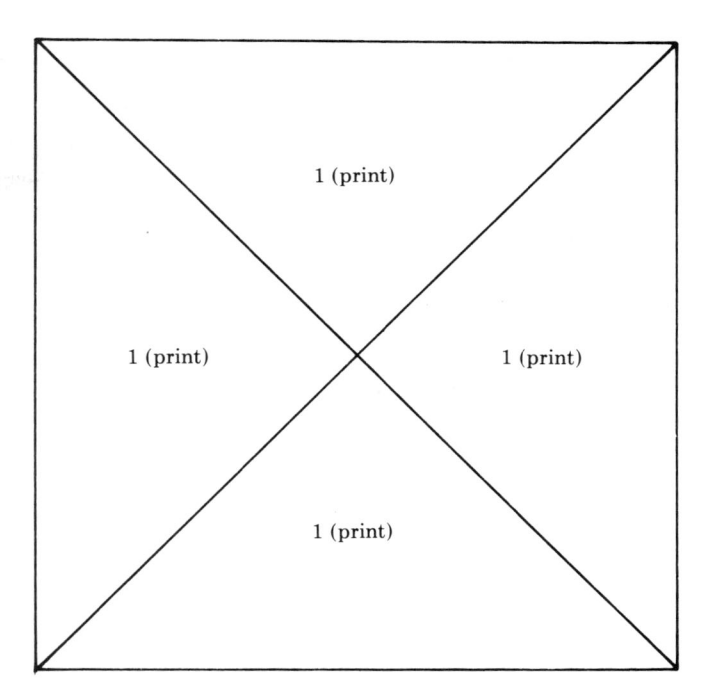

1 (print)   1 (print)

1 (print)

BLOCK DIAGRAM

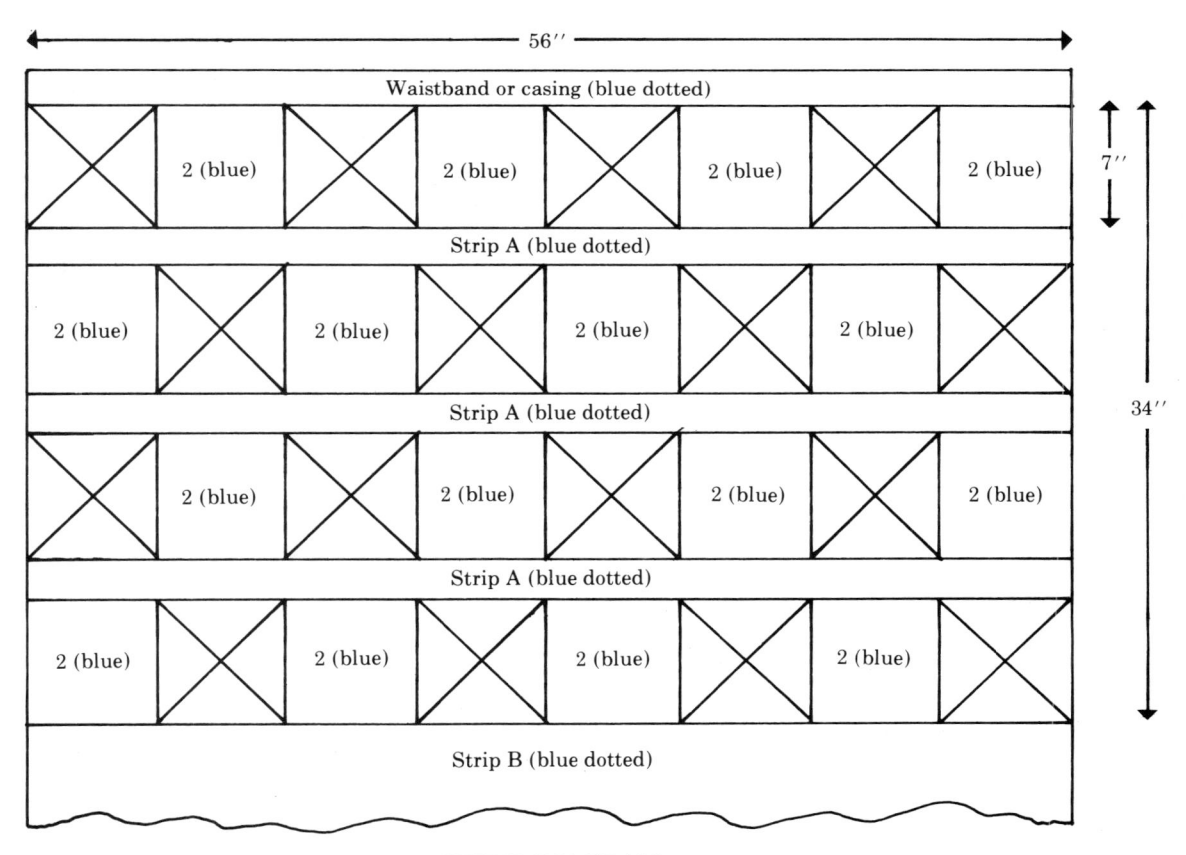

← 56″ →

Waistband or casing (blue dotted)

2 (blue)   2 (blue)   2 (blue)   2 (blue)   ↕ 7″

Strip A (blue dotted)

2 (blue)   2 (blue)   2 (blue)   2 (blue)   2 (blue)

Strip A (blue dotted)

2 (blue)   2 (blue)   2 (blue)   2 (blue)

Strip A (blue dotted)

2 (blue)   2 (blue)   2 (blue)   2 (blue)   2 (blue)

Strip B (blue dotted)

34″

SKIRT DIAGRAM

21

Squares and Triangles Skirt

There are two versions of this skirt; both versions use the same templates.

MATERIALS AND EQUIPMENT

Skirt fabric: (*Version 1*): 3/4 yard black print; 1 1/2 yards red; 1/4 yard blue dotted swiss; 1 yard blue.
(*Version 2*): 1 5/8 yards black print; 1/2 yard red; 3/4 yard orange dotted swiss; 5/8 yard green gingham.
Lining fabric: 1 3/4 yards.
Sharp scissors, pencils, straight pins, needles, zipper or elastic, sewing thread.

DIRECTIONS

Before beginning the skirt, read the general directions on pages iii to v.
1. Cut out the appropriate templates on plates 19 and 20.
2. Cut out the required pieces listed below.
3. Following the skirt diagram for the version of your choice, assemble the squares, triangles and strips.
4. Measure the completed skirt and cut the lining material to match.
5. Sew the sides of the skirt together, and sew the sides of the lining together. If you are planning to use a zipper in the skirt, be sure to leave the appropriate opening at the top.
6. Lay the wrong side of the lining on the wrong side of the skirt with the top edges of the skirt and the lining even. Sew the skirt and lining together 1/4" from this top edge.
7. Following the directions in the introduction, apply either the elastic casing or the waistband to the skirt.
8. Hem the skirt and the lining separately.

VERSION 1
NUMBER OF PIECES TO BE CUT

Piece No. 1 . . . . .12 Black Print (BP)
Piece No. 2 . . . . .24 Red (R)
Piece No. 3 .18 Black Print (BP)
Piece No. 3 . . . . .18 Red (R)
Piece No. 3 . . . . .36 Blue Dotted Swiss (BD)
Strip A (3 1/4" × 54 3/4") . . . . .4 Blue
Strip B (54 3/4" × sufficient width to give desired length plus 3 1/4" for the hem) . . . . .1 Red

VERSION 1   VERSION 2

Waistband (3 3/4" × the desired length) . . . . .1 Blue
or
Elastic casing (3 1/4" × 53 3/4") . . . . .1 Blue

VERSION 2
NUMBER OF PIECES TO BE CUT

Piece No. 1 . . . . .12 Black (B)
Piece No. 1 . . . . .6 Red (R)
Piece No. 2 . . . . .12 Orange Dotted Swiss (O)
Piece No. 3 . . . . .36 Orange Dotted Swiss (O)
Piece No. 3 . . . . .18 Red (R)
Piece No. 3 . . . . .18 Black (B)
Strip A (4 3/4" × 54 3/4") . . . . .1 Black
Strip B (2 3/4" × 54 3/4") . . . . .2 Green Gingham
Strip C (54 3/4" × sufficient width to give desired length plus 3 1/4" for the hem) . . . . .1 Black
Waistband (3 3/4" × the desired length) . . . . .1 Black
or
Elastic Casing (3 1/4" × 54 3/4") . . . . .1 Black

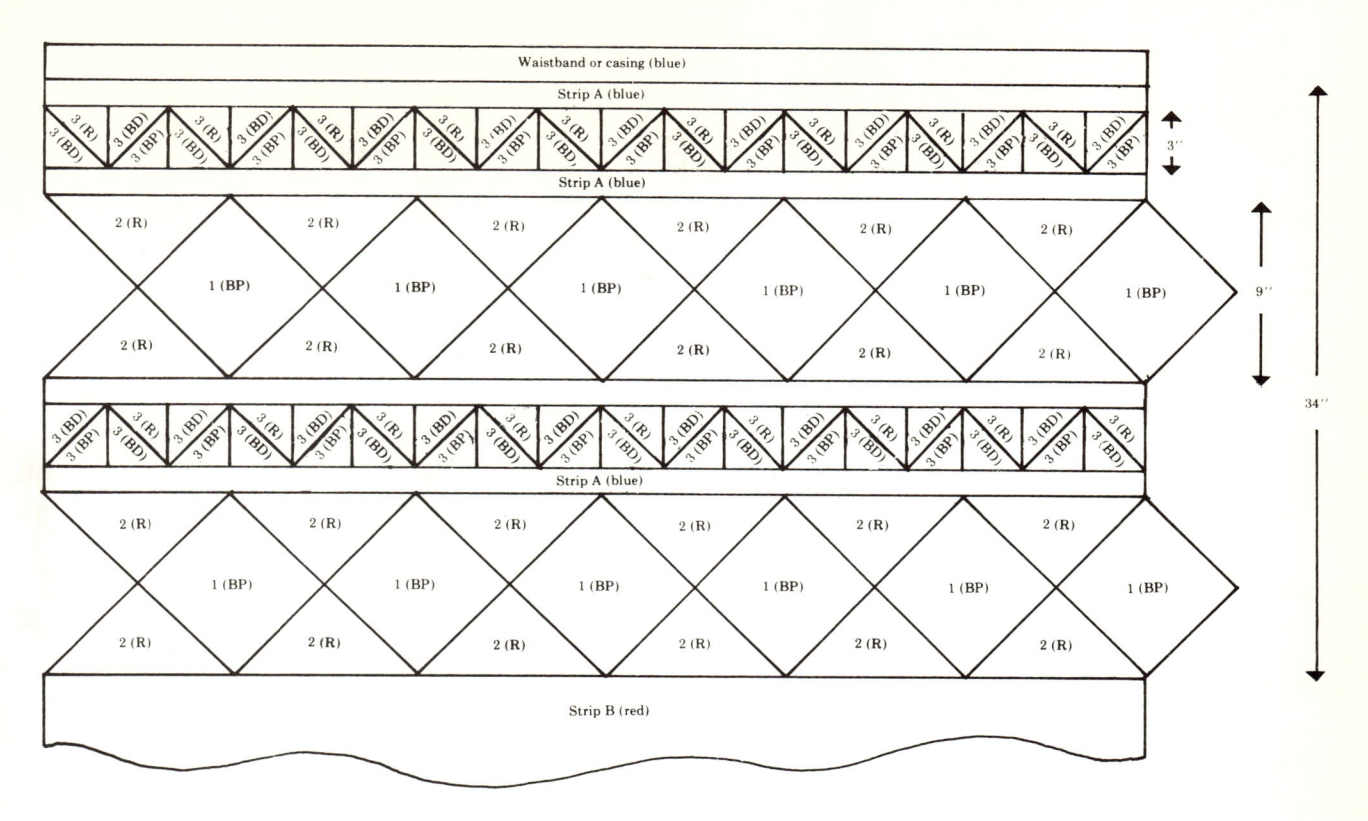

VERSION 1 SKIRT DIAGRAM

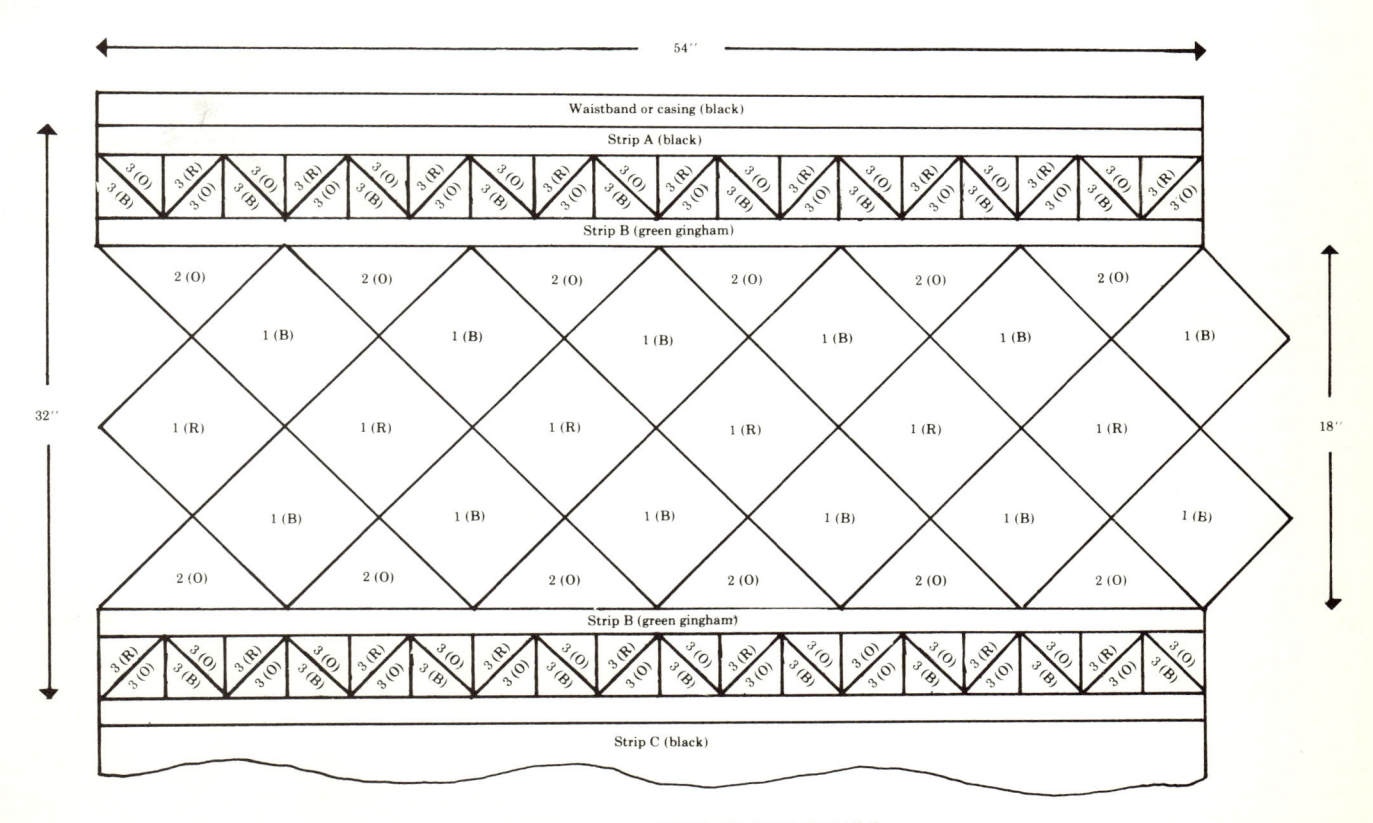

VERSION 2 SKIRT DIAGRAM

23

Broken Dishes Skirt

MATERIALS AND EQUIPMENT

Skirt fabric: 3/4 yard blue print; 3/4 yard pink; 1 yard pink dotted swiss; 1 7/8 yards blue dotted.
Lining fabric: 1 7/8 yards.
Sharp scissors, pencils, straight pins, needles, zipper, sewing thread.

DIRECTIONS

Before beginning the skirt, read the general directions on pages iii to v.
1. Cut out the appropriate template on plate 21.
2. Cut out the required pieces listed below.
3. Following the diagram for Block I, sew the pieces into twelve blocks.
4. Following the diagram for Block II, sew the pieces into twelve blocks.
5. Following the skirt diagram, assemble the pieced blocks and the strips.
6. Measure the completed skirt and cut the lining material to match.
7. Sew the sides of the skirt together, and sew the sides of the lining together. Be sure to leave the appropriate opening at the top for the zipper.
8. Lay the wrong side of the lining on the wrong side of the skirt with the top edges of the skirt and the lining even. Sew the skirt and the lining together 1/4″ from this top edge.
9. Following the directions in the introduction, apply the waistband to the skirt.
10. Hem the skirt and the lining separately.

NUMBER OF PIECES TO BE CUT

Piece No. 1 . . . . .48 Blue Print
Piece No. 1 . . . . .48 Pink
Strip A (2 1/4″ × 64 3/4″) . . . . .4 Pink Dotted Swiss
Strip B (2 3/4″ × 64 3/4″) . . . . .2 Blue Dotted
Strip C (64 3/4″ × sufficient width to give desired length plus 3 1/4″ for the hem) . . . . .1 Pink Dotted Swiss
Waistband (3 3/4″ × the desired length) . . .1 Blue Dotted

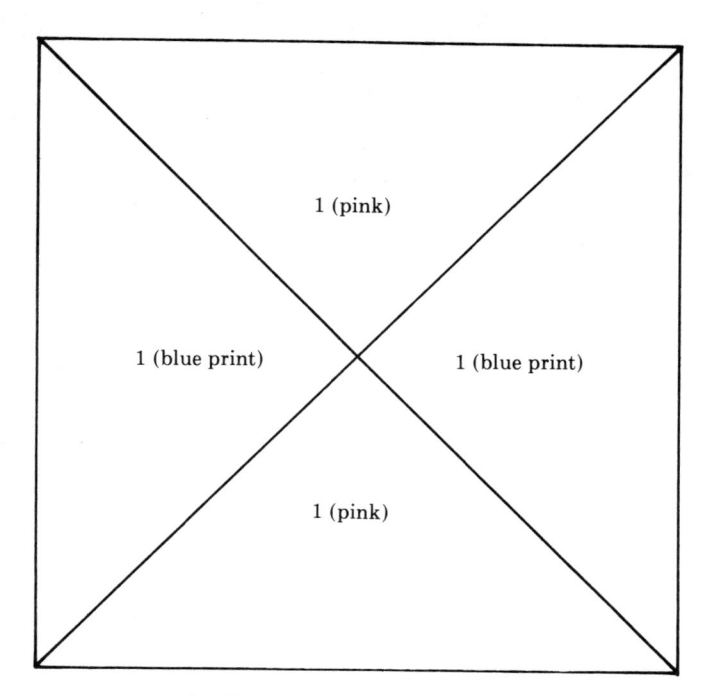

BLOCK I DIAGRAM

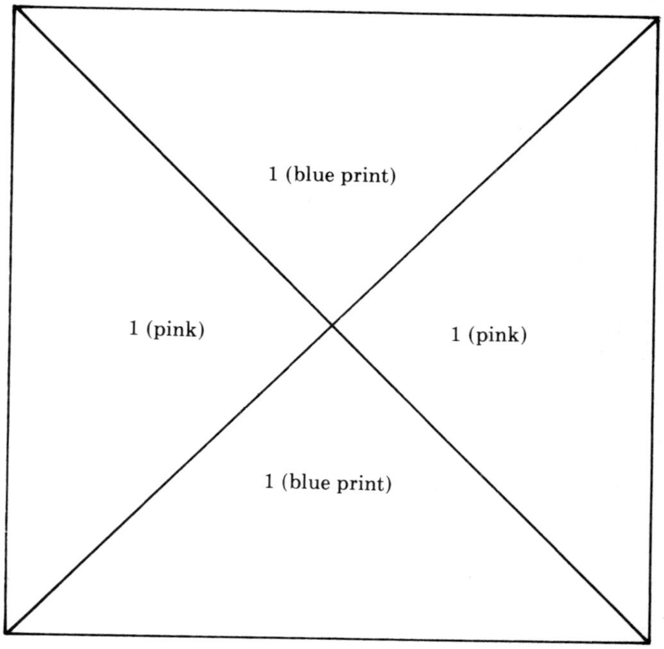

- 1 (pink) — top
- 1 (blue print) — left
- 1 (blue print) — right
- 1 (pink) — bottom

BLOCK II DIAGRAM

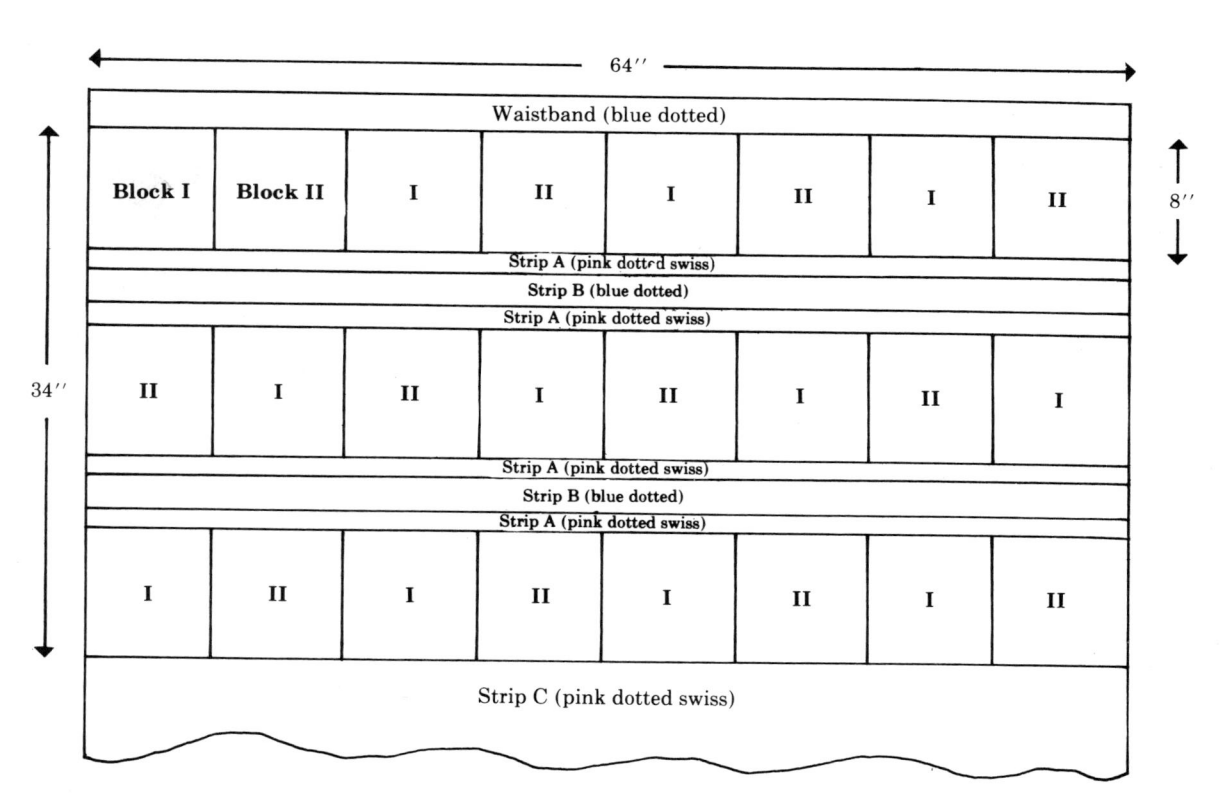

- 1 (blue print) — top
- 1 (pink) — left
- 1 (pink) — right
- 1 (blue print) — bottom

SKIRT DIAGRAM

64″ wide, 34″ tall, blocks 8″

Waistband (blue dotted)

Row 1: Block I, Block II, I, II, I, II, I, II
Strip A (pink dotted swiss)
Strip B (blue dotted)
Strip A (pink dotted swiss)
Row 2: II, I, II, I, II, I, II, I
Strip A (pink dotted swiss)
Strip B (blue dotted)
Strip A (pink dotted swiss)
Row 3: I, II, I, II, I, II, I, II
Strip C (pink dotted swiss)

25

DOVER BOOKS ON QUILTING, CROCHET, KNITTING AND OTHER AREAS

Natural Dyes and Home Dyeing, Rita J. Adrosko. (22688-3) $2.25

Appliqué Old and New, Nedda C. Anders. (23246-8) $2.75

The United States Patchwork Pattern Book, Barbara Bannister and Edna P. Ford. (23243-3) $2.75

State Capitals Quilt Blocks, Barbara Bannister and Edna Paris Ford (eds.). (23557-2) $2.50

Braiding and Knotting, Constantine A. Belash. (23059-7) $2.00

Encyclopedia of Victorian Needlework, S.F.A. Caulfeild and Blanche C. Saward. (22800-2, 22801-0) Two-volume set $12.00

The Complete Book of Doll Making and Collecting, Catherine Christopher. (22066-4) $4.50

Design and Make Your Own Floral Appliqué, Eva Costabel-Deutsch. (23427-4) $2.50

Knit Your Own Norwegian Sweaters, Dale Yarn Company. (23031-7) $3.25

Easy-to-Make Felt Ornaments, Betty Deems. (23389-8) $3.00

Smocking: Techniques, Projects and Designs, Dianne Durand. (23788-5) $2.00

Easy-to-Make Bean Bag Toys, Jane Ethe. (23884-9) $2.50

Easy and Attractive Gifts you Can Sew, Jane Ethe and Josephine Kirshon. (23638-2) $3.50

Early American Patchwork Patterns, Carol Belanger Grafton. (23882-2) $3.00

Geometric Patchwork Patterns, Carol Belanger Grafton. (23183-6) $3.00

Traditional Patchwork Patterns, Carol Belanger Grafton. (23015-5) $3.00

Patchwork Playthings with Full-Size Templates, Margaret Hutchings. (23247-6) $2.00

Teddy Bears and How to Make Them, Margaret Hutchings. (23487-8) $5.95

The Standard Book of Quilt Making and Collecting, Marguerite Ickis. (20582-7) $4.95

Easy-to-Make Dolls with Nineteenth-Century Costumes, G.P. Jones. (23426-6) $2.95

Filet Crochet: Projects and Designs, Mrs. F. W. Kettelle. (23745-1) $1.75

First Book of Modern Lace Knitting, Marianne Kinzel. (22904-1) $3.50

Paperbound unless otherwise indicated. Prices subject to change without notice. Available at your book dealer or write for free catalogues to Dept. Needlework, Dover Publications, Inc., 180 Varick Street, New York, N.Y. 10014. Please indicate field of interest. Each year Dover publishes over 200 books on fine art, music, crafts and needlework, antiques, languages, literature, children's books, chess, cookery, nature, anthropology, science, mathematics, and other areas.

Manufactured in the U.S.A.